Hearing God's Whisper:

Discovering the Sacred in Ordinary Moments

Sheri LaCava Dursin

TwinWizards
PRESS

Published by Twin Wizards Press
ISBN: 978-0-9988336-1-3
Library of Congress Control Number: 2020913406
Hearing God's Whisper/Sheri LaCava Dursin
Paperback | *Twin Wizards Press,* 2020

Scriptures taken from the Holy Bible, New International Version®, NIV®. Copyright © 1973, 1978, 1984, 2011 by Biblica, Inc. ™ Used by permission of Zondervan. All rights reserved worldwide.
www.zondervan.com The "NIV" and "New International Version" are trademarks registered in the United States Patent and Trademark Office by Biblica, Inc. ®

Additional Scripture quotations are taken from The Living Bible copyright © 1971. Used by permission of Tyndale House Publishers, a Division of Tyndale House Ministries, Carol Stream, Illinois 60188. All rights reserved

Cover design by Rosie Henderschedt.
Cover photo by Josefin on Unsplash.com.

www.hearinggodswhisper.com

DEDICATION

For Mark,
Charlie and Alex,
the joys of my life.

CONTENTS

Introduction vii

Seeking God 11

Listening To God 31

Resting in God 41

Trusting in God 55

God's Love 73

Letting Go 85

Everyday Spirituality 97

An Allegory of Five Gardens 117

Seasonal Reflections: Advent and Christmas 131

Seasonal Reflections: Lent and Easter 143

Prayers for Everyday Grace 153

Works Cited 174

Acknowledgements 175

About the Author 176

INTRODUCTION

When I was on retreat many years ago, the speaker said something that changed the course of my spiritual journey: *"Don't ever be satisfied with where you are with God at this moment. Always desire something deeper."* I was struck with the realization that it is our desire to encounter God that defines our journey of faith. We set out, longing to find God and hear God's voice. If we remain open to an intimate and deepening relationship with our Creator, we'll begin to encounter God in new ways.

If you picked up this book, it is my hope that you are longing to get to know God a little better. Perhaps you've been having trouble connecting with God because of outside factors or past experiences.

What methods have you been using to connect with God in your life? Where has your spiritual journey taken you so far, and what are the roadblocks you've encountered along the way? These are important questions to ponder for anyone who is seeking God and finding themselves in a rut or a spiritually dry place.

The earliest seeds of this book were planted when I was a senior in college and attended my first spiritual retreat—a five-day silent retreat on the shores of Rhode Island. Together with 25 of my classmates, we were guided by our retreat leaders through the Spiritual Exercises of St. Ignatius Loyola, a week of silent, contemplative practices designed to help each of us deepen our relationship with God. This was my first experience of spirituality as a practice...something you set out to do, rather than something that was handed down to you by your parents, religious leaders, or other outside influences.

This practice shaped my faith life for many years to come, culminating in my own retreat ministry that I've developed over the past twelve years. The very first retreat I presented was called "Hearing God's Whisper," which I created with Annie, my dear friend and partner on the journey. We talked about the importance of pausing in our busy lives to embrace quiet and stillness. In the stillness we can begin to hear God's whispers in our lives. We can open ourselves to the mystery of God's plans for us. We can find God in the ordinary moments of each day. It was a message that resonated deeply with every woman who attended the retreat. We all felt the desire for "something deeper" in our relationship with God.

My parish retreat ministry led to an online ministry, through the world of blogging...something that felt like a natural coming together of my spirituality and my love of writing. This book is a compilation of six years of blog posts, each one a reflection on our journey of faith. Each blog post is meant to serve as a mini-retreat—a few minutes to step away from the distractions of life to reflect on God's love. For the most part they consist of stories and observations from my daily life: my morning commute, my son's piano recital, a summer vacation, a conversation with a friend, a church choir rehearsal—all ordinary places where I encountered something sacred and heard God's whispers.

In this book, the essays or reflections can be read in any order, and many of them have questions for reflection or activities to further enhance the "retreat" experience at home. They are organized into the following themes: Seeking God, Listening to God, Resting in God, Trusting God, God's Love, Letting Go, and Everyday Spirituality. The book also contains a five-part original "Allegory of Five Gardens" as well as seasonal reflections for Advent, Christmas, Lent, and Easter. The book closes with a series of original prayers and poems for everyday moments.

The first step in engaging with the reflections and prayers in this book is to view them as an invitation from God. A reminder that God is present and close, and wanting a deeply intimate and personal relationship with each and every one of us. If you begin by accepting this important premise, it is my hope that you'll hear God whispering to you through the words on these pages.

The next step is to believe and trust that God is at work in your life. This can be done by pondering your own creation and realizing the stunning truth that *you were created to be loved by God*. God knows you better than anyone. God lives in you and has a plan for your life that is unfolding each and every day.

Contemplating our faith is not an academic exercise. It can be done by taking a closer look at the very ordinary moments in our lives. In these pages, you will be encouraged to find yourself in a sandcastle, a spider web, a bountiful garden, a frustratingly slow computer, or a pair of smudged sunglasses. God is present in all that we do, and if we are open to the invitation, we can find God anywhere.

It is also important to remember that spirituality is not static. It is constantly changing and evolving, and it is something that we continue to practice over a lifetime. Our faith lives change from day to day and from season to season. Remember, there is no finish line when it comes to a relationship with God. There is always "something deeper."

My prayer for you is that in some small way, my words will give you new eyes to see the beauty of God's creation, new ears to listen for God's whispers, and a new outlook to experience the transforming power of God's love.

PART ONE:
SEEKING GOD

Seek the Lord where he may be found;
call on him while he is near.

ISAIAH 55:6

Thin Places

Would you consider yourself a seeker?

Do you find yourself always on the lookout for God, longing to know more about Him, longing to find Him and to hear His voice? Celtic Christianity has a wonderful concept called "thin places." According to this belief, a "thin place" is one where the veil between heaven and earth is lifted. God's presence is so strongly felt, that the human and the divine are only separated by a very thin space. Because Ireland is full of such beautiful natural landscapes, many of these thin places were believed to be sacred places in nature. The cliffs, the ocean, the rocky landscape.

But thin places can be found anywhere—a comfy chair on your back porch, a hidden path through the woods, a busy city street. And thin places can also be found in moments of time: the birth of a child, a family celebration, a moving liturgy, a beautiful song, or an experience helping someone in need. The important thing is that when you encounter one of these thin places, you experience an encounter with God. My husband has always said he feels closest to God among the mountains of Vermont, with their green brilliance and lofty peaks.

Seekers are often full of questions: Why? What does God want? What should I do? What is God's will? Seekers will turn to God with concerns about moral dilemmas and difficulties with particular aspects of our faith. The important thing (and to me, very comforting thing) to know is that God embraces our questions. He wants us to come to Him with everything we have...even our doubt. The goal of truly knowing God is one that will never be fully realized in this life. I AM WHO AM. God is ultimately unknowable, but our journey to seek and learn about God is where we find meaning in life.

However...

Sometimes we grow weary of seeking. Sometimes all we want is to be found. Or there may be times that we get derailed in our search for God. Stress...Worry...Suffering. All of this can get in the way of our efforts to seek the Lord. In a homily at my parish years ago, Fr. Stan Kennedy, M.S. gave a wonderful reflection on the parable of the Lost Sheep.

> *"Jesus is the Good Shepherd. It is not the job of the sheep to go off looking for the shepherd. And so as believers, we have one simple job...to be found."*

During times of stress or suffering, we need to forget about our seeking and embrace God as our home. God knows us intimately and loves us unconditionally and we don't have to do any work for that to happen. All we have to do is let God wrap His loving arms around us and welcome us home. And if we consistently invite God into our everyday experiences...He will find us.

QUESTIONS FOR REFLECTION

1. At what times do you identify with the seeker? Where do you go to seek out God?

2. Reflect on some of the "thin places" you've discovered in your faith journey.

3. When are the times when you simply long to be found? How does God represent "home" for you?

Responding to God's Invitation

"Stop in anytime!"
"My door is always open."

I've never felt comfortable with these kinds of open invitations. They're much too vague and raise way too many doubts for me. *What if I choose a bad time? What if they don't really mean it? Maybe I'll put it off for now. They're not really expecting me, so I won't go today.* It becomes too easy to let time fall away and never really take advantage of the invitation.

I've always preferred something more formal. An invitation addressed specifically to me with a specific date/time and specific details of the event, so I know what to expect. (As you can see, I'm big on specifics!)

We are told that God invites us into an intimate relationship with Him. Again, this sounds a bit vague. How do we take advantage of this invitation? When and where do we show up? What is expected of us? The following is my attempt to make God's invitation a bit more personal and...specific!

WHO

Make no mistake...God is directing this invitation to *you*. Not to a general group of chosen people to which you may or may not feel you belong—but to you. Our Lord says: "I have called you by name. You are mine" (Isaiah 43:1). God promises that He will never forget us, for He has written our names on the palm of His hand (Isaiah 49:16). John's Gospel introduces Jesus as the Good Shepherd, caring for each of His sheep in a deeply personal way. "The sheep hear his voice and come to him; and he calls his own sheep by name and leads them out" (John 10:3). What a powerful thing to realize that this invitation from God—through His Son Jesus Christ—comes to each of us so individually. Close your eyes for a moment and imagine God calling you gently and sincerely by name. You are a child of God...and you matter!

14

WHERE

Interestingly, our holy invitation does not direct us to God's house, although we may visit there every Sunday. But our connection to God takes place within our own hearts. Through the gift of the Holy Spirit, God abides in us; and for our faith to flourish, we have to let God in. There's a famous depiction of Jesus standing outside a door...but there is no doorknob on the outside. It is based on the Scripture from Revelations 3:20: "Here I am! I stand at the door and knock. If anyone hears my voice and opens the door, I will come in and eat with that person, and they with me." God respects our free will. Jesus will not enter unless we let Him in. He is always there, waiting for us, but it is up to us to open the door.

WHEN

Our invitation from God is for now! Today. Right when you put down this book. It is a daily call to keep Jesus with us always. God should be invited into every moment of our day. If this is still too vague or overwhelming to contemplate, then look for ways to make it more specific. Plan "dates" to be with God. Set aside a few minutes each morning to pray or read Scripture. Attend a spiritual retreat. Take advantage of any spiritual programs offered by your parish. Spend some time in silence each day.

WHAT TO BRING

All you need to bring is an open heart. A willingness to let God in. A desire to be connected to God in all that you do and say. A willingness to live out the teachings of Jesus in your words and actions. Jesus tells us, "I am the vine; you are the branches. If you remain in me and I in you, you will bear much fruit; apart from me you can do nothing" (John 15:4).

My prayer for you today is that you accept God's invitation. That you live in God's love just as God lives in you. Amen.

Show Me the Way

I've never liked driving to new places.

For the longest time, whenever I had to go somewhere I had never been before, I would follow the same procedure. I'd look up the directions, write them out in giant print so I could read them in the car, try my best to memorize them, and head out, still a bit nervous.

Realizing this fear was keeping me from trying new things and seeing new places, I examined the reasons why I was so reluctant to venture out to places I'd never been. Two reasons stood out to me.

I like to know where I'm going.
I hate getting lost.

All of this changed with the availability of GPS and smartphones. I now had a navigator to help me get where I wanted to go! The very first time I used my GPS was to visit my friend Rebecca at her new home in a nearby town.

I quickly discovered that a successful trip required three things of me. I had to LISTEN. If my radio was up too loud, I wouldn't hear the spoken directions. I had to BE AWARE. The GPS voice wasn't going to tell me if a small child suddenly ran out into the road. And I had to TRUST. Could a space-based satellite navigation system really help me find the way?

Hesitantly, I set out for her house, and as promised, I was led right to her door, exactly where I wanted to go. What freedom! Suddenly my world held no more boundaries. I could travel anywhere, as long as I had my trusty GPS to guide me.

How might our lives change for the better if we trusted God to be our navigator? And why do we often find it so difficult to do? It's human nature to want to know where we're going. To want to be our own pilot. We are creatures of control. It takes a tremendous leap of faith to set off on a journey without knowing the way. So how do we do it? How do we surrender enough to let God lead the way?

By doing three things:

LISTEN

Just as I had to turn down the radio to hear the GPS instructions, we need to be still and silent once in a while in order to hear God's call. Clear away the noise and distractions of life. "Be still and know that I am God" (Psalm 46:10).

BE AWARE

God often speaks to us in very surprising ways, and distractions are all around us. Take stock of who and what is getting your attention these days. Who is God sending to speak to you today? Who or what is standing in your path, leading you away from God?

TRUST

We must believe that God wants only the best for us. "For I know the plans I have for you," says the Lord. "They are plans for good and not for evil, to give you a future and a hope" (Jeremiah 29:11). We need to trust in God's plan instead of insisting on our own plan.

Jesus said to his disciples, "I am the way, the truth, and the life. No one can come to the Father except through me" (John 14:6). He promised to make a place for us in heaven and to show us the way. But He never promised that it would be a straight course. Don't be surprised if your path changes when you least expect it.

When I left Rebecca's house at the end of our visit, for reasons unknown to me, the GPS decided to send me home another way. I immediately became anxious. *But I know the first way now! That's how I want to go.* But GPS had another plan for me. That is how God works in us. Just when we feel secure that we are on our way—on a path that is righteous and true—God sends us on another way.

We have no choice but to follow with anticipation, excitement, and faith. Secure in the knowledge that it will lead us to the Promised Land.

QUESTIONS FOR REFLECTION

1. Which part of following the path towards God do you find the most challenging—listening, being aware, or trusting?

2. Can you think of a time you trusted God's navigation in your life, even when it took you off the path you had mapped out for yourself?

Fully Known By God

Who is the person in your life that knows you best?

Most of us reveal ourselves to others in bits and pieces. Depending on the setting, the circumstances, or the nature of the relationship, we let people see only parts of us. We hold back things that we don't want others to see, for any number of reasons. For most of us, it is a rare few individuals that truly know us. And even then, there might be things we still keep to ourselves, even from those we are closest to.

In Psalm 139 we encounter a God who knows everything about us. When we sit and stand. A God who knows our every thought and where we are at every moment. A God we cannot hide from...who is always there.

> *I can never be lost to your Spirit! I can never get away from my God! If I go up to heaven, you are there; if I go down to the place of the dead, you are there.*
>
> PSALM 139:7-8

When I was young, the idea that God knew everything about me made me nervous and uncomfortable. It felt like someone was reading my diary. With my immature understanding of sin, I felt like God was watching me, waiting for me to do something wrong or make a mistake. I wondered if God was listening in on my unkind or jealous thoughts. I could pretend to be this perfect person to those around me, but God knew the truth.

I didn't like that feeling.

Perhaps you still feel that way. Catholic guilt is very real! Our images of God from childhood—as a stern judge or a scolding parent—stay with us through the years.

As I matured in my faith, I no longer saw God as an administer of shame but as a source of mercy and forgiveness. Gradually the idea of being fully known by God was something that I welcomed. Now it gives me incredible comfort. The act of surrendering all that I am to God feels like the strongest safety net. The firmest foundation.

I encourage you to challenge the view you may hold of God as a judge, who only makes an appearance in our lives when we do something wrong. A picture of God waiting to dole out punishment. A God who is trying to "catch us" in moments of sin. Challenge this view and spend some time with the God who created you, chose you, blesses you, and calls you.

What does it mean to be known by God?

> *How precious it is, Lord, to realize that you are thinking about me constantly! I can't even count how many times a day your thoughts turn toward me. And when I waken in the morning, you are still thinking of me!*
>
> PSALM 139:17-18

You were created to be loved by God. When you are feeling alone, and hopeless, God is there...loving you still. God offers us prodigal mercy and radical grace. More than we deserve or could ever earn. When you struggle with doubt or fear, bring those feelings to God, who will not flinch from your angriest thoughts or your most desperate questions.

To be fully known and still fully loved is an incredible gift. You don't have to earn it. It's not like getting picked for a sorority, being chosen for a job, or having someone choose you on an online dating site. God wants to know each and every one of us. We are His beloved children. His chosen ones. Our names are written on the palm of His hand.

Your name is written on the palm of God's hand.

As you ponder this amazing thought, my prayer for you is that you will surrender to God, who knows you and loves you unconditionally. A love that is beyond measure. A love that is faithful and unshakable. Live in that love. Wake up each morning telling yourself: "I was created to be loved by God." Amen!

REFLECTION ACTIVITY

Write the following words in bright colors on an index card or Post-It Note:

"I was created to be loved by God."

Pin it up on your bathroom mirror, your coffee maker, or your computer...somewhere you will see it first thing in the morning. Hold that thought with you as you move through each day.

Finding God in the Storm

My God, my God, why have you abandoned me?

We hear this well-known scripture verse at the cross, when the Earth was covered in darkness, and Jesus uttered these words moments before he surrendered his spirit and died. But that's not the first time we hear it; the line first appears in Psalm 22. Although the specific reason is not known, the author of the Psalm is clearly suffering. "My God, my God, why have you abandoned me?" The passage goes on to say:

> *Why are you so far from saving me, so far from my cries of anguish? My God, I cry out by day, but you do not answer, by night, but I find no rest.*
>
> PSALM 22:1-2

Have there been times, when you've felt like the author of this Psalm...that God was very far away? Perhaps during a time when you were experiencing personal suffering. Or maybe from the nagging worry that suffering may be just around the corner. We live in a world full of uncertainty and fear. Worries about our personal health and well-being and the well-being of our family members. Worries about the economic climate...will we keep our jobs? Can we "stay afloat" financially? Worries about global threats, war, and violence—global pandemics, social injustice, mass shootings, and natural disasters.

How easy it would be to collapse under the weight of all these worries. How often do we feel like that's exactly what we might do? How does this fear manifest itself? Sleepless nights, stress, anxiety. Living in this state of perpetual worry...how do we pray?

Dear God, *please* don't let me get sick.
Dear God, *please* don't let anything happen to my children.
Dear God, *please* don't let me lose my job.

We lovingly and a bit desperately bring our laundry list of fears to God...praying that He will protect us from anything bad. *Dear God, don't let this happen!* We fear that if the worst did happen, we wouldn't be able to handle it.

These troubling times can make us feel like we're in the middle of a raging storm... beaten down by winds and rain, feeling like we might drown or be swept away. In the everyday trials and tribulations of life, the storm may not seem as life-threatening, but it still can be relentless and exhausting. The Scripture that always comes to my mind when I'm in the middle of one of these stormy times comes from Mark's gospel:

> *That day when evening came, he said to his disciples, "Let us go over to the other side." Leaving the crowd behind, they took him along, just as he was, in the boat. There were also other boats with him. A furious squall came up, and the waves broke over the boat, so that it was nearly swamped. Jesus was in the stern, sleeping on a cushion. The disciples woke him and said to him, "Teacher, don't you care if we drown?" He got up, rebuked the wind and said to the waves, "Quiet! Be still!" Then the wind died down and it was completely calm. He said to his disciples, "Why are you so afraid? Do you still have no faith?" They were terrified and asked each other, "Who is this? Even the wind and the waves obey him!"*
> MARK 4:35-41

It comforts me to know that the disciples behaved exactly like I would have in this situation. They were scared! They wanted the storm to go away. They didn't trust that they would survive it. Jesus was right there in that boat with them...but still they didn't trust. And can you really blame them? Here they were, caught up in a "furious" squall, and Jesus was *sleeping on a cushion?* I love this translation, because that image of Jesus fast asleep on a comfy cushion perfectly captures the way the disciples must have been feeling. That God was far away. *"My God, my God, why have you abandoned me?"*

Children love this Bible story, because it's exciting. They can picture being out on that stormy sea, and how awesome it was that Jesus calmed the storm with a simple gesture of His hand. It really shows His power and might. They see Him as a superhero. What I'd like to suggest to anyone who focuses on the 'Jesus as Superman' aspect of the story, is that maybe we're missing the point. Those disciples weren't going to survive because Jesus calmed the storm...they would survive simply because He was with them. He would keep them calm and safe and secure in the midst of the storm. That's what Jesus wanted His disciples to realize and that's why He called their faith into question. I think the same point holds true for us today. What we should take away from this gospel reading is not that Jesus is here to calm the storms in our lives and make them go away. We don't need Jesus to do this in order to survive, although, admittedly, it would be nice! Instead, we need to know and truly believe that Jesus is with us in the midst of every storm, to help us get through it.

So maybe, instead of going through the laundry list of prayers that nothing bad will happen to us, we should simply pray that God will be with us if and when it does. For reasons we will never understand, God doesn't always take away the storms in our lives. He gave us a world with free will, human choice, science, and laws of nature. What God can promise is to help us weather the storm. To ride it out. To get through to the other side, where the sun will once again shine upon our faces.

QUESTIONS FOR REFLECTION

1. When you are experiencing a "stormy" time in life, how do you pray?

2. Does is change your approach to challenges knowing that Jesus is with you in the midst of every storm?

Finding God in the Construction Zone

A few years ago, I had to pass through a major construction zone on my way to work in the morning. The road was being torn up, sidewalks were temporarily gone, and the two lane road was funneled down to one. It was a huge hassle that started my day with stress and irritation.

Each morning, as my car was inching its way past this road work, I would see a woman bravely walking through the mess. Wearing a bright pink track suit and a big smile, she wove her way past bulldozers, police cars, traffic cones, and broken chunks of asphalt. I could see that this morning walk was part of her daily routine, and she wasn't going to let a little construction stop her. I admired her. If it were me, I would have immediately used this as an excuse to stop walking for the many months it might take to finish the road!

Does your life ever resemble a chaotic "construction zone"—filled with mess and upheaval? What happens to your faith life during this time? Do you find it difficult to pray, to find quiet time to be alone with God? Or maybe you're so focused on the problem at hand that you forget about God's presence in your life.

Years ago, I was scheduled to go on a weekend retreat with some women from my parish. Some unexpected things came up at home, and I felt I couldn't "afford" the time away. At the last minute I cancelled my reservation in order to stay home and take care of things. In doing this, I was failing to take care of myself. It resulted in my feeling even more stressed and overwhelmed. I often wonder if I had gone on the retreat, would my approach to solving those problems been clearer and more effective?

How often do we set aside our faith until a time when conditions are more ideal for prayer and communion with God? *Once things have calmed down in my life, I'll get back to praying. Right now I just have to get through this.*

This is the exact opposite of what we should be doing! It is precisely our faith that will sustain us through those "under construction" times.

A few minutes of quiet prayer can make all the difference. Inching your way through the chaos with Jesus by your side can make the journey less burdensome and arduous.

God is here for us, waiting to guide us safely through to the other side. We only need to lean on Him.

I think of Jesus, facing the sick, hungry, and needy...believers numbering in the thousands. He would often slip away from the crowds, to retreat into the wilderness to pray. "Yet the news about him spread all the more, so that crowds of people came to hear him and to be healed of their sicknesses. But Jesus often withdrew to lonely places and prayed" (Luke 5:15-16).

Jesus knew that He needed time to be alone with God. I imagine He would come back from those moments of stolen prayer refreshed, with a renewed sense of purpose, confident that He walked this journey with His Father. It was vital to the continuation of His ministry. We can and should follow His example. Keep on walking. Bring Jesus with you. Let God guide you.

As I waited for the construction work to be completed on my commute, I looked forward to seeing this woman walking on a smoother path. It gave me hope that she persevered through the muddle and would now have an easier road to travel.

It gave me courage to keep on walking.

Drifting Towards God

I have a friend who was a social worker at an elementary school, and she spent a lot of time talking to her young students about the peaks and valleys of friendship. Children's loyalty can change with the wind. A best friend one day can be an icy acquaintance the next. This can lead to confusion and hurt and can be very difficult to navigate. To help her students make sense of it, my friend used the metaphor of two drifting boats. It's ok to drift away from a friend for a while, if that's what seems best. It doesn't mean you can't come back together at some future point.

More than anything, God desires to be in relationship with us. But the metaphor of the drifting boats isn't quite right in describing this divine relationship. God never drifts away from us, but is instead the constant fixed point, firmly anchored in a place of love and faithfulness. We may come and go depending on our feelings, emotions, doubts, and life circumstances...but the best news is that God never moves. We can always drift back (or even come crashing back!) onto the shores of God's love.

In her book *Journal Keeping: Writing for Spiritual Growth*, Luann Budd poses the question: "On a scale of 1-10 (10 being intimate), how close do you feel to God today?" Sit for a few minutes in silence and answer this question. Write down the number.

Spend some time examining why you scored yourself that way. If your number is on the low side, why might that be? Have you drifted away from God for some reason? What is holding you back from moving closer to God? Very often, it's guilt. Or maybe confusion. A feeling that God has abandoned you during a time of need. Or it may be a fear of revealing yourself. *If God truly saw me for everything I am, God couldn't possibly love me!*

Recognize that these thoughts may be natural and very human, but they are not based in the truth of God's love. Try to spend a little bit of time each day pondering God's unconditional love, acceptance, and presence in your life. You'll find your thoughts begin to change, and you'll drift closer to God each day.

If you scored high on the scale, that's great! You're feeling close to God in this moment. Drink it in and let yourself be filled with gratitude. Examine the circumstances that have you feeling so close to God right now. What methods are you using to connect with God in your life?

- Maybe it's nature. You're in touch with the beauty of God's creation. You find God in the warm sunshine, the gentle breeze, the endless ocean, the enduring woods.

- Maybe it's relationships. You feel fulfilled by the love in your life, and you know that God has placed these people in your path. You feel God every time you hug your child, smile at your spouse, laugh with your sister, or cry with a friend.

- Maybe it's your ministry or vocation. You are doing God's work, and you feel a sense of fulfillment and purpose. You can hear God speaking to you through the work that you do...helping others, caring for the earth, tending to the needs of God's Kingdom.

Whatever the reason may be, lean into it. Capture the feeling. Write about it in your journal. There will come a time when you inevitably drift away again, and it will help to have a reminder of this time when you felt close to God's radiant love.

And remember, our spiritual practice is constantly changing and evolving. Your score today may not be your score tomorrow. Return to this exercise again and again in your ongoing journey to draw closer to God.

God is Waiting for You

Some of my fondest memories from my teenage years are the nights I would come home after an evening out with my friends. My mother always waited up for me, and my return home had a lovely sense of ritual to it. I would come in and join my mother on the couch, and she would ask to hear every detail of my night out. Sometimes my stories were filled with joy, other times heartache and high school drama. More often than not, they were probably pretty boring. It never made any difference to my mom. She listened with total focus and rapt attention. How wonderful it felt to know that she cared not only about me but about every facet of my life.

I can't help but compare this memory to a doctor I used to see years ago when I was in my 20's and living in Boston. She would breeze into the examining room and spend as little time with me as she possibly could. She was a nice woman, but it was obvious she was overbooked and had other patients waiting. I didn't doubt her skills as a physician, but I never really felt like she cared about me or what I had to say. It got to the point where I felt guilty asking her questions about my health...believing she had more important or sicker patients to deal with than me.

Which of these two examples matches more closely with your image of God? When you approach God in prayer, do you do so with comfort and confidence or with a sheepish sense of apology? *"I don't mean to bother you, but..."*

It's easy to believe that God is too busy to hear us. How many billion people live on this planet? Why would God care about the details of one little soul? The answer is simple.

Because God created you, and you belong to God.

Our relationship with God is one of constant invitation. Like my mom sitting on that couch, God is always waiting, eager to hear from us, no matter what we have to say. God is strong enough to bear it all: our complaints, our doubts, our fears, our anger, our sorrows, our joys, our moments of transformation. Nothing is too dark or too trivial or too overwhelming for God's loving ears.

There are many different ways to pray, but one that I love the most is just talking to God. It brings home for me the fact that God is not a remote power, too busy or lofty to hear from us. God is present and close, and wanting an intimate relationship with each and every one of us.

My prayer for you today is that you will truly believe that God cares for you and is waiting to hear from you.

REFLECTION ACTIVITY

Spend 10-15 minutes today talking to God just like you would talk to a close friend.

PART TWO:
LISTENING TO GOD

God speaks in the silence of the heart.
Listening to God is the beginning of prayer.

SAINT TERESA OF CALCUTTA

Symptoms of a Tired Soul

What is the most tired you've ever been?

This question is very easy for me to answer...because I am the mother of twins. My boys are grown now, but it seems like just yesterday that I brought them home as infants. I remember a lot of joy from their first year of life. Quite honestly there's a lot I think I blocked out! But one thing I remember with crystal clarity is how tired I was. Eight feedings a day times two. Endless diaper changes. Mounds of laundry. Plus all the anxiety and fear that comes along with being a brand new mother. For me, it gave new meaning to the word exhaustion—a tiredness that went straight through to the very marrow of my bones.

I remember when my boys were about six weeks old, I had to have very minor out-patient surgery, but it required general anesthesia. The nurses wondered why I was so excited to be put under. I answered with a desperate laugh, "Just let me sleep as long as you possibly can!" The kind of rest I needed in those days was rest for my body. The meeting of a biological need with very clear physical symptoms.

How do you know when you are in need of *spiritual* rest? What are the symptoms of a tired soul? We live in a world where busy lives are the norm. Whether it's for work, for family, for church, or even for fun...we're constantly on the go. If you think about your lifestyle at this point in time, would you describe it as a state of "being" or a state of "doing"?

When I was ten years old my family moved to a new house that had a pond in the front yard. It was quite an ecosystem—frogs and turtles moving in and out of the water, and ducks swooping down and landing with a splash. Added to the mix were the frequent landings of soccer balls or basketballs in the water, an endless stream of skipping stones, and even one time my little sister! As a result, the pond was always murky. Because the water never had a chance to be still, you could never really see clearly through to the bottom. This is what our lives look like in a constant state of doing. They become cloudy and churned up. It becomes difficult to see God. To focus on what's really important.

This murkiness is one of the symptoms of a tired soul. Our spirits need to rest, to give that water time to settle. Otherwise we're always going to be struggling to see clearly.

Another way of measuring the state of our souls is by noise level. How noisy is your life? Distractions and chaos can make it very hard to hear and almost impossible to listen. Living in a state of doing is like having a constant hum of white noise in the background. It becomes difficult to really hear God. And we know from Scripture that God isn't always going to shout to be heard. Sometimes He speaks in a whisper.

> *"Go out and stand before me on the mountain," the Lord told Elijah. And as he stood there the Lord passed by, and a mighty windstorm hit the mountain; it was such a terrible blast that the rocks were torn loose, but the Lord was not in the wind. After the wind, there was an earthquake, but the Lord was not in the earthquake. And after the earthquake, there was a fire, but the Lord was not in the fire. And after the fire, there was the sound of a gentle whisper. When Elijah heard it, he wrapped his face in his scarf and went out and stood at the entrance of the cave.*
>
> 1 Kings 19:11-13

In order to hear God's gentle whisper, we need to come away to a quiet place. To shut out the world of distractions and really listen. Just as a physically tired body needs sleep to feel rested and restored, one who is spiritually tired needs quiet and stillness.

The practice of listening becomes a starting place where God will come to you in the stillness and whisper to you. That's where you will hear words of love and messages that are unique and meant for your ears alone.

The Language of Silence

16th century mystic John of the Cross once wrote, "Silence is God's first language." I'm a firm believer that God comes to us every day in any number of ways, through the bubbling laughter of our children, the joyous harmony of a choir, the hustle and bustle of a busy day, even the anguished cries of a broken heart.

But there's something special about silence.

Silence is our gift to God. A "sacred pause." A time to stop what we're doing and listen. To soak in God's presence and allow ourselves to be filled up. In the words of Mother Theresa: "Silence of the heart is necessary so you can hear God everywhere—in the closing of the door, in the person who needs you, in the birds that sing, in the flowers, in the animals."

Years ago, I facilitated a women's faith group at my church and each time we met, we would take 15 to 20 minutes of quiet reflection. It was our "alone time" with God. (For many of us busy women, it was the only alone time we would get!) To set the mood and help us focus on our prayer, I'd gotten in the habit of playing soft instrumental music. One time, I forgot my music, and so our quiet reflection time was held in complete silence. I was amazed at the difference! The silence was so rich. My spirit felt alive to the moment, and I allowed myself to be still and reach a deeper connection with God.

How often do you experience silence or stillness? It may not come naturally to us at first. Silencing our outer world is the first challenge. Turning off the TV. Sneaking away from the demands of our families, even if just for a few moments. Putting away our phones. Ah...the biggest challenge yet! (Put it in another room if you have to. Every time your text alert beeps or vibrates, it's going to pull you back out of your silence. Why tempt yourself in that way?)

The second and much more difficult challenge is to silence your inner world. Quieting the mind is not easy! Distractions tend to creep in. The pressures of the day cling with stubbornness. You can't stop thinking about that difficult conversation you had at work today. You can't stop worrying about the report that's due tomorrow. You wonder how your children are doing, or your aging parent.

My suggestions for achieving interior silence is to begin with a prayer.

> *Dear God, I desire to sit in silence with You, but I'm*
> *bringing a lot of noise along with me. Please help me*
> *set my thoughts aside. I'm giving them over to You so I*
> *can listen for Your voice in the silence.*

If it helps, actually imagine yourself picking up each distracting thought and placing it into God's hands.

After that, it's ok to let your mind wander. Focus on a passage from Scripture, a poem, or a particular question. Or just open yourself up to God's inspiration and invitation. Use your thoughts, imagination, and emotion to really *be* with God, and follow where God is leading you. Don't stop and analyze each thought or feeling. Just keep meandering through this time with your Creator. This is often where the best insights come from.

If you have time, use a journal to record the thoughts that came to you during your time of silence. If you make a habit of this, you can look back over your insights and search for patterns. That's when you know God is really trying to tell you something.

REFLECTION ACTIVITY

Sometime before this day ends, take three minutes to sit in complete silence. Sit on your bed or your favorite comfy chair...even in your car. Any place that you can find quiet. Don't try to accomplish anything during those three minutes. Just be with God and see what happens.

An Act of Surrender

Seeing that I had forgotten my choir music at rehearsal one evening, my friend held her music between us so I could look on with her. I was puzzled by a note she had written in the margins of her sheet music: *"Listen to Sheri."* I asked her what it meant, and she explained that at a previous rehearsal she had struggled to find a note in a particularly challenging chord. Hearing that I had it, she wrote that message to herself as a reminder to listen to me. I chuckled at her answer, saying, "Listen to Sheri...that's pretty good advice for all things in life, isn't it?"

So often the voice that guides us in our lives is our own. The inner voice that dictates our plans and goals. That maps out our path to success or victory. Putting it simply...most of the time we think we know best. Like the former President who once said, "I am the decider!"—we're convinced that our way is the best way. We even become frustrated when those in our lives (hint, hint...our children!) don't listen to us. Controlling everything around us becomes a defense. Our control is the only thing we feel is keeping us together, when perhaps it's the very thing holding us back from truly growing in our faith.

Listening to God begins with an act of surrender.

If we are committed to listening to God's call in our lives, we need to surrender. To give up our need to control, to manage, to decide, to be in charge.

Thy will be done.

When Jesus approached Simon and Andrew, casting their nets on the shore of the Sea of Galilee, he offered them an invitation. "Come, follow me," Jesus said, "and I will send you out to fish for people" (Matthew 4:19). The two brothers immediately dropped their nets and followed him...and their lives were changed forever.

It takes practice—listening to God. Letting God lead us and guide us might not come naturally at first. But we must remember that God has chosen us and comes to us with an invitation. How will we respond? Are we open to the mystery of God's plans for our lives? Complete surrender is not an easy thing. In battle, surrender signals defeat. It implies a loss of control and a giving up or giving in. To surrender to an enemy is a failing act of last resort.

But to surrender to God's loving plans is something else altogether. Our ego-driven belief that we know best falls away as we begin to trust God. "For I know the plans I have for you, says the Lord. They are plans for good and not for evil, to give you a future and a hope" (Jeremiah 29:11).

To surrender to God means...

1. to love God with your whole heart, mind, and soul
2. to trust that God is working in your life and
3. to believe that God will meet all of your needs.

This *loving* and *trusting* and *believing* can be done through prayer and examination. Ask God what it is in your life that is most in need of your surrender. To what are you gripping too tightly? What nets do you need to let go of so you can follow Jesus?

Thy kingdom come; thy will be done.

It's during these moments of surrender that the deepest listening takes place. If we open ourselves to the invitation with unclenched fists and open hearts, we'll be ready to discover God's plans for us.

And ready to follow wherever God may lead.

Filtering out the Background Noise of Life

Last year I signed up for a weekly yoga class during my lunch hour. The class was called "Sweat and Surrender," and I thought it would be the perfect break to de-stress from my day and return to work relaxed and rejuvenated. The class was great, and the instructor was gentle and encouraging. There was only one thing preventing me from enjoying it...the very loud Zuumba class held in the room next door!

Yoga takes concentration. You need to focus and listen—both to the instructor and to your own body as you move through the different postures. The Zuumba music was so distracting, I could never reach this level of focus. I tried my best to ignore it. To tune it out. But I just couldn't.

We all move through life with varying degrees of "background noise." We try our best to tune it out, but it can become a significant challenge to hear—and really listen—to the voice of God. The noise is always there to distract us, pulling us away from the calm, the stillness, and the focus we need to listen to our Creator.

Can you identify the background noise in your life? For most of us, it begins with the general hectic pace of today's world. We get used to it until we don't realize how truly "noisy" our lives have become. It's so important to retreat once in a while. To escape from the noise and be still. Silence and breathing, both of which I write about in this book, are excellent ways to minimize the background noise of a busy life.

Maybe the background noise you struggle with is negativity. Fear is always there, waiting to drown out any truths we might hear from God about trust, about God's faithfulness, about God's promises, and about the knowledge that God is carrying us and caring for us always. Negativity can build up inside us like an automatic response, until it becomes a thick wall that blocks out God's messages in our lives. It takes practice, but you can intentionally turn your thoughts towards God when you feel negativity creeping in.

And finally, our own Inner Critic can be a damaging source of background noise. Telling us we're never going to be good enough, the voice of the Inner Critic is loud and constant and very hard to turn off. But if we're aware of it, we can recognize it and name it and begin to strip this voice of its power. And once you do, you'll be better able to listen for the Voice of Truth—the Voice of your loving God. The Voice that says you are loved and accepted exactly the way you are!

Listening is such an important part of our spiritual practice. When we pray, we do a lot of talking *(Please! Thank you! Help me! Do this!)* If you can be still and quiet long enough, you'll begin to hear God speaking to you.

I recently joined a new yoga class. It meets in the evenings in the library of an elementary school. The room is quiet and peaceful with dim lights and an inspiring, gentle-voiced instructor. It's just what I was looking for...but never would have found if I didn't make the decision to leave the noisy environment of my old class.

REFLECTION ACTIVITY

Take some time this week to examine the background noise of your life. What's the "Zuumba music" that might be preventing you from hearing God's whisper? How might you minimize that noise and focus on what really matters?

Part Three:

Resting in God

Come to me all who are weary and
burdened, and I will give you rest.

Matthew 11:28

Practicing Spirit-Care

Do a Google search on "self-care," and you'll come up with over two billion hits. It's a popular buzzword these days, and I've seen it described in lots of different ways in countless blogs, websites, and articles. According to the *Oxford Dictionary*: "Self-care is the practice of taking an active role in protecting one's own well-being and happiness, in particular during periods of stress."

Most often self-care is recommended for people who spend the majority of their time taking care of others. Teachers, nurses, social workers, health care aides, and those who work in caring ministries. The truth is, we can all benefit from self-care, but many of us are reluctant to do so. We think of it as a luxury. Something we don't have time for. Some of us even feel that self-care is selfish. *There are too many people that need me! How can I take time away from my important work to do something for myself?*

What if instead of calling it self-care, you called it spirit-care? Does it seem more worthwhile? Isn't it important to care for your spirit as a beloved child of God? Wouldn't God want that for you?

Perhaps it would make you feel better to realize that this was something Jesus often did. He recognized when he needed to pause, to step away and take time to restore himself. He knew that if He was going to be able to do God's will, He needed to be able to listen, pray, and to spend time alone with God.

- From Luke 6:12—"One of those days Jesus went out to a mountainside to pray, and spent the night praying to God."

- From Mark 1:35—"Very early in the morning, while it was still dark, Jesus got up, left the house and went off to a solitary place, where he prayed." (He did this after spending the night before healing many sick and driving out demons.)

- From Luke 5:15-16—"Yet the news about him spread all the more, so that crowds of people came to hear him and to be healed of their sicknesses. But Jesus often withdrew to lonely places and prayed."

- From Matthew 14:23—"After he had dismissed them, he went up on a mountainside by himself to pray." (He did this after feeding the crowd of 5,000.)

I love the fact that through his own actions, Jesus Himself gives us permission to retreat. Spiritual retreats have long been my favorite method of spirit-care. I've often heard it described as a "sacred pause." From the very first retreat I attended—a five-day silent retreat when I was in college—I was amazed at how life-changing it could be to press pause on my busy life in order to focus on uninterrupted time with God. The importance of retreats became the hallmark of my own retreat ministry.

I think some people struggle with the idea of self-care because it seems too much like pampering...this sense that you're doing something that completely and only benefits you, as if you are more important than anyone else. But when you retreat, you aren't alone. You're spending this time with your Creator. Spirit-care is a partnership. Spirit-care renews us so we can continue our important work of caring for others. Your spirit needs to be filled up from the inside out. Cars can't run on empty. Watering cans can't give life to plants if they're dry.

You need to be filled up before you can be poured out.

Spirit-care can be relaxing, peaceful and restorative. It can be deep, wild, and creative. It's different for each person. But it doesn't just happen. Remember, the dictionary describes it as taking an "active role." I like to think of it as a practice. Something you work on over time, because you value yourself. Because you believe that you are worth it, and the work you do needs the very best of you.

Just Breathe

Then the Lord God formed man of dust from the ground, and breathed into his nostrils the breath of life; and man became a living being.

GENESIS 2:7

We all have those days when nothing seems to go right. When we're stressed out, or preoccupied, or wound up. We can't get out of our own way. Our bodies are tense, our shoulders hunched, our faces scrunched into a permanent frown. Like a rubber band stretched so tight we're about to snap, we feel as far from "holy" as we can get. And sincere prayer seems impossible in the mood we're in. The words won't come and we can't force them.

It's ok.

On these days your prayer can be as simple as breathing. Stop what you're doing and just breathe. Plant your feet solidly on the ground. Relax your shoulders. Close your eyes. With each breath, focus only on the air moving in and out. Fall into a rhythm as you breathe slowly and deeply.

Breathe in God's love, grace, and mercy.
Breathe out your worries and doubts.
Breathe in God's presence.
Breathe out your frustrations and defeats.
Breathe in the cleansing power of the Holy Spirit.
Breath out negative thoughts and ill feelings.

Using breath as a form of prayer is an ancient Christian practice. The Hebrew words for "breath" and "spirit" are the same. When we're breathing, we call forth the Holy Spirit that dwells within us. We're using our bodies to focus on the essence of our connection with God. Our own moment of Divine creation when God breathed the breath of life into our nostrils.

The focused rhythm of breathing is really all that's needed to center you and bring you closer to God. But if you'd like to add a bit more, choose a simple phrase to repeat as you breathe.

God is with me.
Holy Spirit, guide me.
Do not be afraid.
Be still and know that I am God.

Because breathing is a constant process in our lives, praying with your breath is a wonderful way to access God at any time during your busy days, your stressful days, your bored days, or your really, really bad days.

A Road Map to Balance

Are you able to recognize when your life is out of balance? What does it mean...and what does it look like?

It often happens gradually, and most of the time we are so caught up in the daily rush of life, that it wouldn't even occur to us that we might be out of balance. We work like crazy, pushing ourselves to the limit. We don't realize that our minds are burned out, our bodies are worn out, and our spirits are wrung out.

God created us to live a life of balance.

BALANCE OF BODY

When your body is out of balance, you will eventually figure it out. Lack of sleep catches up with you. Poor nutrition can sap you of energy. Not drinking enough water can lead to headaches and even dizziness. This idea of balance can go the other way too. Exercise and healthy eating can become a preoccupation. I've seen athletes push themselves to the point of injury because they didn't pay attention to the signs from their own bodies.

BALANCE OF MIND

A friend of mine told a story of a particularly busy time working long hours for weeks on end because her job required it. She gave herself no breaks and took no time to rest her mind or recharge her batteries. She came home from work one night, and her husband offered to pick up dinner. "What would you like?" he asked her. "Choose your favorite takeout restaurant, and I'll go get us something to eat." My friend had stretched herself so thin that she couldn't even make that simple decision. Her brain just couldn't do it. On the verge of tears she looked at her husband and said: "You know what I like. Can't you just choose something?" This was a moment of a life out of balance.

BALANCE OF SPIRIT

When our spirit is out of balance, we tend to overly focus on one emotion or feeling—usually those emotions that do not bring us joy. We fixate on bitterness over love. Guilt over acceptance. Deficit over abundance. Fear over faith. The backdrop of our spiritual life can also fall out of balance. Solitude can lead to loneliness. Crowds can become overwhelming. If we put all our focus on doing one thing, our spiritual life will feel off kilter. Faith calls for us to live through prayer and action. Through time in solitude and time in community.

God desires us to live a life of balance.

Once we discover that we are out of balance, how do we get back on track? How do we achieve this balance in our lives? After you finish reading this reflection, take out a piece of paper and write down the following four questions:

1. What is important in my life?
2. What are some things I absolutely need in life to feel happy?
3. What brings meaning to my life?
4. What makes me feel inspired?

Over the next few days, weeks, or even months, spend some time pondering your answers to these questions. Write them down so you can refer back to them. This is your road map to balance. Anything you do that brings you closer to the things you've written will center you. Anything you do that drives you away from these things requires further examination.

We may not always have a choice. We have obligations in life that bring stress and exhaustion and we can't change that. But we can make smaller changes to weed out some things that are not important. To diminish that which does not bring meaning to our lives. And to lean into that which inspires us.

The changes might be internal. (Gently changing our thoughts.) They may be external. (Seeking out friends who help us achieve this

47

balance.) They may be faith-based. (Asking God in prayer to help us stick to the things that really matter.) It's an evolving, constantly changing process. We move toward balance, we fall out of balance, we move back again. But we know that in this journey towards balance, God is with us every teetering and steady step of the way.

The Happy Minute

In my never-ending quest to be healthier, I recently dusted off an old exercise DVD to get myself moving. Toward the end of the 30-minute workout, the instructor talks about the "happy minute"—the moment when the music changes to a slower beat to begin the cool down. For someone who hadn't exercised in a while, this definitely was a happy minute for me!

Such a lovely phrase with its focus on a very small measure of time. So often our thoughts and worries span decades. Looking ahead to the struggles of soon-to-be aging parents, or kids leaving for college. Will there be money to retire? Will our health sustain? Will we lose our jobs to another round of layoffs? This straining ahead causes us to miss what's happening around us in the present moment. We forget to recognize the happy minute when we're in it.

One day when my boys were teenagers, I was cleaning the kitchen, listening to them playing Super Smash Bros™ on our Wii. They were laughing and screeching and having a ball. I stopped for a minute and realized how much time I had been investing lately worrying about their futures. Grades, homework, college applications, driver's licenses, careers, friendships, relationships. I pushed those thoughts away. *In this moment, they are happy.*

Think back to the last time you paused long enough to recognize one of these moments. Where were you, and what were you doing? The happy minute often occurs when we are with loved ones, sharing a moment of joy or connection. Other times we may experience it in solitude, appreciating a beautiful view or listening to a lovely piece of music.

It's easy to miss these moments altogether. There are so many things that threaten to pull us out of the present. It takes awareness and practice to hold onto the happy minute and truly savor it.

In the hit song "Little Wonders," Rob Thomas calls them "small hours," and they are true—often hidden—blessings. Not just the big landmark events, but the little moments in between, in which God enters the quiet spaces of our hearts and whispers joy into our souls. As Thomas goes on to say: "Time falls away, but these small hours...these small hours still remain."

REFLECTION ACTIVITY

Take time every day this week to stop, reflect, and be thankful. Look for the happy minute. Keep a notebook handy where you can record these moments so you can come back to them later. Try to do this several times a day until it becomes a habit.

My Summer Goal...To Just Be

Every year in June, with summer vacation about to begin, bringing a sense of endless promise and boundless time, my husband and I spend a lot of time talking about goals. "What do you want to accomplish this summer?" I ask him. "What are your top three goals for the summer?" he counters. We even imposed these goals on our boys. What activities should they pursue this summer? How would that help them achieve long-term success? What is one major personal goal they could accomplish before school starts up again in the fall?

Goals are good and important and can lead to certain kinds of growth. But this constant focus on "doing" has its pitfalls. We live in a world that values accomplishments and achievements. We present ourselves to the world as living resumes, saying: *"This is what I do"* as opposed to *"This is who I am."* Our lives need to be efficient and productive at all times. We devote ourselves to the gods of progress and success. This approach to life can easily backfire and end up blocking true and meaningful growth. We miss out on opportunities to build relationships, to grow in our closeness with God, to experience the sacred in the everyday moment.

In a world filled with the demands of so much DOING, perhaps summer, with its warm, gentle breezes and long, hazy days of sunshine, should be a time for just BEING.

- BEING wise enough to know when we need to rest and restore ourselves. This is not a luxury or a guilty pleasure but a vital necessity! It's not laziness, but a time of being spiritually alive and tuned in to the ways in which God is moving in our lives.

- BEING open to an intimate and deepening relationship with our Creator. A constant pursuit of doing makes it difficult to hear God and respond to His stirrings in our souls.

- BEING available to experience the sacred in the most ordinary present moment. Pay attention to what we might be missing. The thing that will have the most impact on us today is most likely not on our daily "to do" lists.

- BEING aware of friendships or relationships that need nurturing. Practice the art of doing "nothing" with our spouses, kids, or friends. Take time for idle conversation and see what's revealed in the process. Talk, but more importantly, listen.

- BEING able to sit in the silence and let ourselves be filled up by the presence of God.

- BEING humble enough to realize that God's plans for us are so much more important than our own personal goals for success.

- BEING creative in our approach to spirituality as we strive to deepen our relationship with God. Try something new this summer. Attend a spiritual retreat or workshop. Keep a journal of thoughts on "being." Discover a new way of praying.

Let's put our resumes of accomplishment away for a few months each summer. Or better yet, let's rewrite them altogether. What we "do" should be an outpouring of who we "are" and who God wants us to be. Who we are is the core of our being and the foundation of our lives. Don't we deserve time to nurture and cultivate that part of ourselves? It shouldn't be pushed to the back burner to be replaced by lists of things we feel we must do and accomplish. Our connection to the Divine should dictate our "to do" list.

Spend your summers BEING a child of God.

How Healthy is Your Spirit?

We hear so often about the importance of wellness of body, mind, and spirit. We visit a doctor for our annual check-up. We measure the health of our bodies through blood work, cholesterol tests, EKG's, etc. We have assessments for measuring different aspects of our brain and intellect. But how often do we give our spirit a check-up? How often do we ask the question: "How healthy is my spirit?"

Try this little exercise. Read each statement below and say whether you agree or disagree:

- I feel like I know myself well.
- I accept and love myself even though I am not perfect.
- Everything in life has something to teach us.
- Overall, people are good and kind.
- I feel loved.
- I am able to forgive and forget.
- There is a lot of beauty in the world.

Now do the same thing for this next set of questions:

- Life is full of struggles that I have no control over.
- I am constantly doing and running with a checklist.
- I tend to hold grudges with those who have wronged me.
- There are many things about myself that I wish I could change.
- I feel alone and on my own.
- I soothe myself with food, alcohol, or something else from the outside world.
- I've had a lot of bad luck in my life.

For which set of statements did you answer "I agree" the most? If it was the first set, your spirit is very strong, indeed! People with a healthy spirit have a positive, loving view of self and others. They believe in the inherent goodness of the world. They're able to get through a crisis and remain strong in their beliefs. They have a strong faith life and a deep connection to the sacred.

If you agreed more with the second set of statements then there's a good chance your spirit has some wounds that need healing. People with a wounded spirit focus more on their flaws and imperfections. They tend to have a negative outlook on life. They often view themselves as a victim and look to blame others—or God—during a time of crisis. They believe there's little meaning behind what happens in the world.

Having a wounded spirit doesn't make you a bad person. It just means you're a bit further away from wholeness. Why is it important to worry about spiritual wounds? They can affect your daily life just as much as a physical injury. A few years ago I injured my foot and required months of physical therapy. It was amazing how this chronic pain seeped into every area of my life. I became irritable and despondent. I put on weight. I had no energy. The same is true of spiritual wounds. They fester, affecting how you look at the world and interact with others. They prevent you from seeing what it is you need to be happy, healthy, and productive. They block you from living up to your potential and being the person you were meant to be.

It's so important to nourish your spirit if you want to move toward wholeness. Begin with some honest soul searching. Identify factors in your life that have led to your spiritual wounds. Ask God for the grace to help you heal. Focus on what's really important to you and what brings meaning to your life. Spend some time in silence or meditation. Take time for relaxation. Do something just for you...it's not a luxury, it's vital! Share your stories with people you trust. Pray.

Spirituality is not static. It changes from day to day and through different stages of life. Take some time today to check in with your spiritual health.

PART FOUR:

TRUSTING IN GOD

God does not ask you not to feel anxious,
but to trust in Him no matter how you feel.

THOMAS MERTON

The Unfailing Faithfulness of God

The beginning of a new year is a season marked by change. We come up with a list of resolutions...things we want to change about the way we live our lives. Our health. Our habits. Our goals and dreams. My sister and I like to call this month Jan-NEW-ary.

But the passage of time can also bring unwelcome change. Sickness, job loss, a change in relationships or circumstances. When this occurs, the ground shifts beneath us, and we feel unsteady—unsure of what lies ahead. Change that is unplanned can lead to stress, anxiety, and a host of other uncomfortable feelings, all of which are rooted in fear.

During times like this, it helps to remember something that will never change.

> *Know therefore that the Lord your God is God; he is the faithful God, keeping his covenant of love to a thousand generations of those who love him and keep his commandments.*

DEUTERONOMY 7:9

One of my best friends experienced a great deal of loss in her life over a short period of time—losing two dear friends to cancer followed by the death of her father. Not knowing how best to comfort her, I sent her a card with one simple phrase:

"I'm not going anywhere."

I wanted her to know that she could count on me. That I would be there for her. The solid ground she could cling to when so much else was slipping away. I couldn't bring back her loved ones, but I could offer her my presence. I could be loyal and steadfast. I texted her several times a day for weeks on end, hoping she would trust in my promise. It didn't seem like much at the time, but she later told me how much it helped her, just knowing I was there.

God is just like that. The most loyal friend you've ever had. The One who will always stand by you, no matter what. The One who welcomes you with open arms no matter how long you've been away or out of touch. The One who always tells you the truth, sticks up for you, and loves you exactly the way you are.

> *He has given us both his promise and his oath, two things we can completely count on, for it is impossible for God to tell a lie. Now all those who flee to him to save them can take new courage when they hear such assurances from God; now they can know without doubt that he will give them the salvation he has promised them.*
>
> HEBREWS 6:18

Life throws us a lot of curveballs. It's easy to doubt the future. But we never need to doubt God's love for us, God's presence in our lives, or God's plans for us.

God has a plan and a purpose for each of us, but we can't always know how it will unfold. (At times God's plan may seem to directly contradict our own plans!) But we know that God is there to walk alongside us and hold us up, giving us strength and hope. Most importantly, God offers us unconditional love, mercy, and grace. This will never change. We can cling to—and count on—the unfailing faithfulness of God.

My prayer for you today is that you will feel God's presence more strongly than ever before. When you fear anything in your life changing or slipping away, picture God whispering to you:

"I'm not going anywhere."

God Picks Us Up When We Fall

For three years my office window looked out over a church parking lot. People used it for all kinds of things. A practice course for school bus drivers in training, a path for neighborhood walkers, an unofficial commuter lot, a place for truckers to park and eat lunch. But my favorite thing to see was parents using the parking lot to teach their children how to ride a bike. What a sweet distraction from my day's work. I could see the fearful looks on the faces of the young riders. I could hear the parents' promises floating up through my office window.

"I won't let you fall!"
"I promise you won't get hurt."

I remember my husband and I saying these exact words to our boys when they first learned to ride, and I'm very sure my dad made the same promises to me. It's what you have to say to get past the fear in your child so they can take that leap.

If we're being honest...these promises are not exactly iron-clad. It's likely our would-be cyclists *will* fall. There's a chance they *could* get hurt. Not too badly, you hope, but it's a real possibility. What you might more honestly say is this:

"If you fall, I'll be there to pick you up."
"If you get hurt, I'll be there to soothe your pain and dry your tears."
"I will ALWAYS be there, no matter what."

For me, there's no better way to describe God's role in our lives. But it took me some time to come to that realization. I used to pray exactly like those scared kids teetering on a bike for the first time. *"Please, dear God, don't let anything bad happen to me...ever!"* I was so afraid of getting hurt that I held myself back from new experiences and new challenges.

Life has taught me that it doesn't work that way. We all fall. We all get hurt. It's part of engaging in the world around us. Living up to our potential involves a certain amount of risk. This knowledge could easily leave us paralyzed with fear. Afraid to lift our feet from their firmly-rooted spots on the ground and peddle like mad.

But the beauty of our faith is that God is *always* there for us. To offer comfort. To dry our tears. To ease our pain. To pick us up no matter how many times we fall.

This knowledge is what frees us to get on that bike and go. To fly. To take a leap of faith. To push ourselves toward our sacred destiny. It's what God wants for us.

One beautiful spring day my son took his brand new bike out for a ride. A run-in with a nasty pothole landed him in the emergency room with a broken wrist, a mild concussion, and many cuts and scrapes. I smothered him with love for weeks after that, giving him all the comfort and gentleness a mother could give...which is a lot! His wrist healed, his bruises faded, and his headaches went away. His worst fears (and mine) about getting hurt had been realized, and overcome. And so, too, we heal from the potholes and pitfalls of life. And we do so with the strength of an amazing God who will never let us fall so far or so deep that we can't get up again...and keep on riding.

Prayers from a Night Worrier

Are you a night worrier? My mother has never had any trouble falling asleep at night. But once in a while, if she's unlucky enough to wake up during the night, that's it for sleeping. She calls them "racing thoughts." Turning, churning, and tumbling in her mind at a pace that won't stop.

What is it about the middle of the night that things always seem so dire? We awake with a feeling of dread. A worry that seemed small during the day seems to blow up in the dark of night. Taking on a menacing shape. Like that monster from our childhood, threatening to creep out from under our beds and grab us in our sleep. Larger problems seem insurmountable, even hopeless.

In the dark we are scared children again. We're alone and helpless. We forget everything we know about God's love and faithfulness. We let fear take over. It becomes impossible to place our trust in God. We focus on the darkness (the metaphorical absence of God's light) instead of the quiet.

But remember...the quiet is the best time for listening. Hear what God is whispering to you:

> *So do not fear, for I am with you;*
> *do not be dismayed, for I am your God.*
> *I will strengthen you and help you;*
> *I will uphold you with my righteous right hand.*

ISAIAH 41:10

I hear God saying: *"Sleep my child. Do not be afraid. I'm right here. There is nothing for you to do tonight. Tomorrow we will face the day together. You are not alone."* It helps to actually imagine God's hands in front of me. Comforting, strong, and gentle. I give my fears a physical manifestation, like a heavy box. At God's invitation I place the box full of worries in His hands.

It's easy to feel that God has left us alone in the dark because we cannot "see" His presence. This is precisely the time to let yourself "feel" His presence. Use your imagination or the comforting ritual of rote prayers to remind yourself...

God is **HERE**
God is merciful
God is compassionate
God is powerful

I am not alone.

Living Water

Have you ever watched a small child try to build a castle out of dry sand? She painstakingly fills her pail with scoop after scoop of powdery white sand. With all her might, she lifts the heavy pail and quickly dumps it over. You cringe a bit, knowing what's about to happen. With hope in her eyes, she lifts up the pail to reveal her creation. Tears of frustration flow as the sand collapses around her, and the castle is leveled to the ground.

She doesn't understand what went wrong. You know the secret, and you want to rush over and tell her. She needs to add water! Wet sand is sturdy and strong. It will hold her castle together so it can stand tall. Without water, she'll never succeed.

The dry sand in this story depicts a life lived apart from God. Dry and dusty, with no strong surface to gain a foothold through the trials of life. This kind of barren life is one we fall into because we choose to distance ourselves from God. It's not something God "does" to us or wants for us. In fact, quite the opposite.

> *For I will pour water on the thirsty land, and streams on the dry ground; I will pour my spirit upon your descendants, and my blessing on your offspring.*
>
> ISAIAH 44:3

Jesus repeats this promise to the worshipers in the temple: "Let anyone who is thirsty come to me and drink. Whoever believes in me, as Scripture has said, rivers of living water will flow from within them" (John 7:37-38).

If we're thirsty, it's not because of an absence of water; it's because we choose not to drink. Or maybe someone needs to help us find the water source. In the same way, when we thirst for God's presence in our lives, it's not because God is truly absent, but because we have drifted away from the source of Living Water.

Jesus describes the gift of the Holy Spirit as water because of its life-giving properties. It sustains us, nourishes us, helps us to grow. It washes us clean and makes us new. God provided a limitless ocean for this little girl who longed to build a sturdy sand castle. It was right there for the taking. In the same way, all we need to do is receive the incredible gift of God's grace.

The next time you feel like things are collapsing in around you, remember the strength that can be found in the "Living Water" of the Holy Spirit. It is the secret to a life filled with deep meaning and abundant blessings.

And it's right there for the taking.

Psalm 23 – A Psalm for the Living

God is our refuge and our hope.

This was the topic I found myself writing about when preparing for a retreat several years ago. In looking for some Scripture to use, I went straight for the Psalms which contain dozens and dozens of references to this kind of loving and protective God. I was immediately drawn to Psalm 23. You know this one:

> *Yea, though I walk through the valley of the shadow of death, I will fear no evil; for You are with me; Your rod and Your staff, they comfort me...*

After considering it for a moment, I quickly rejected it for the purposes of my talk. For most people, this Psalm is too closely associated with funerals, death, and dying. I can still remember the scene from the movie *Titanic* when a priest recites these lines to a group of terrified passengers as the ship sinks further and further into the ocean. As beautiful as it was, I wanted to talk about life. I didn't need a Psalm for the dying.

The very next day, I got a call from my younger sister. She was telling me about a Church service she attended at her parish—a Congregational Church north of Boston. There was a seminarian preaching that day; a young woman who had battled and survived breast cancer. The topic of her sermon was Psalm 23. She described it using these exact words...a "Psalm for the living." A daily reminder that she could turn to God for protection, comfort, rest, and reassurance. Anytime she was feeling anxious or hopeless, she would recite this Psalm. It had a wonderful calming effect on her during her treatment and recovery.

For this young seminarian, the "valley of the shadow of death" was all too real of a possibility. For the author of Psalm 23, the phrase may have referred to the many real dangers that faced the people of that time...perhaps even the actual landscape. The "valley" can mean anything for us today. A worry, a difficult situation, a broken relationship. What this Psalm is telling us is that during these times, when we are lost in the valley...God is with us. Nothing can separate us from the love of God during these dark times. We do not need to be overcome by our fear.

From now on, when you hear the words of Psalm 23, I urge you to think of it as a "Psalm for the living." Daily proof that you are not alone. That your life is blessed with God's mercy and goodness. That the Good Shepherd is leading you on the journey.

PSALM 23

The Lord is my shepherd, I lack nothing.
He makes me lie down in green pastures,
he leads me beside quiet waters,
he refreshes my soul.
He guides me along the right paths
for his name's sake.
Even though I walk
through the darkest valley,
I will fear no evil,
for you are with me;
your rod and your staff,
they comfort me.

You prepare a table before me
in the presence of my enemies.
You anoint my head with oil;
my cup overflows.
Surely your goodness and love will follow me
all the days of my life,
and I will dwell in the house of the LORD
forever.

Unanswered Prayers

Please, dear God, don't let him make any mistakes.

This was my hastily whispered prayer years ago when my eleven-year-old son sat down at the piano to perform in the spring recital. He was playing a difficult piece—one that he had been working on for months. I knew he was nervous. I held my breath as he began to play.

Despite my plea to God, there were several noticeable mistakes in his performance, including one heart-stopping moment where he seemed to lose his place in the music before picking it back up again. My heart fell. My son is a deeply sensitive boy and a perfectionist. I knew he would be devastated by these mistakes. And he was. No matter how many times my husband and I told him he did a great job and we were so proud of him, he wouldn't hear it. With choked back sobs and tears of frustration, he could not get past it.

He wasn't the only one who was frustrated. I had a bone to pick with God. *"Come on! It was a simple request! You can move mountains and part seas! Was it really so impossible to help a boy get through one piano piece?"* I felt rejected and a little bit betrayed. I couldn't understand why God refused to say "yes" to this simple prayer.

Fast forward two years. We were back at the same music studio for another piano concert. My son had chosen an even more challenging piece to perform. He knew it by heart, and he was ready. Before he began to play, his teacher got up to say the following words about my son: "When he chose this piece to learn, as his teacher my first instinct was to talk him out of it, because I thought it would be too difficult for him. But he was determined, and he worked hard. And he taught me a valuable lesson. Never again will I tell a student what they *can't* do."

The lights dimmed as my son began to play. He did a beautiful job...his fingers flying over the keys as the melody filled the room and my heart. His performance wasn't perfect. There were some wrong notes and another prolonged pause as he tried to find his place again. I sighed deeply. *So close!* I guess we're in for another rough afternoon.

When the recital was over I rushed over to my son to give him a hug. He hugged me back, smiled, and shrugged his shoulders. "Did you notice I lost my place for a few seconds there?" To my surprise, he wasn't upset. He was ok with it. What a difference from the wrecked little boy of two years ago! My mind jumped back to that moment when I believed that God had denied my prayer. With sudden clarity, I realized how wrong I was. This was God's answer. This year, this moment, this beautiful evidence of growth in my son. God had been holding him and shaping him and working in him all this time.

I understood. God didn't say "yes" to my prayer that day. But He didn't say "no" either. Instead, His answer was "grow." A lesson in faith to be learned not just by my child, but by me.

QUESTIONS FOR REFLECTION

1. God is always loving us and working in our lives, even if we can't always see it in obvious ways. Think back to the "unanswered" prayers in your own life. Was God really saying no? Or was there a greater plan He had in mind for you?

2. Looking back, did you find an answer came later on? Was it the answer you expected?

What Does it Really Mean to Trust God?

In a culture that values self-reliance and individual freedom, trusting God can be a huge challenge. In a world that has the potential to throw us any number of curveballs, sending our lives into a tailspin in an instant, trusting God takes a lot of effort.

Yet, every once in a while, you come across one of those people who doesn't seem to be plagued by these worries. They put their full trust in God. *I trust that God will handle this situation.* For so many years, I never understood these people, or their unflappable belief that all would be well. *Why aren't you worrying about this!* Their calm statements that "God would provide" often felt like platitudes to me. Just something people say. They couldn't possibly mean it all the time.

What if God *doesn't* provide? What if all *won't* be well?

So I went out in search of an answer to this question..."What does it really mean to trust God?" And I was led to the Hebrew word "Aman" which is used over 100 times in the Old Testament. What better place to start than the Hebrew Scriptures that serve as the foundation of our faith.

Aman, means "to be firm or sure; to be certain; to believe." To me, that means that we can be absolutely sure of God's unlimited power, wisdom, and promises. God will never change. The circumstances of our lives may change in ways that are uncertain and scary, the people in our lives may change in ways that are unpredictable and confusing, but God's love and faithfulness do not change. It was this kind of faith that the disciples in Mark's Gospel needed as they faced the storm that threatened to swamp their boat (Mark 4:35-41). Aman. They needed believe that God was with them.

How often I can identify with the disciples in this way, needing to find this kind of faith over and over again. Almost 20 years ago, my husband, Mark, was teaching English at a local high school. He had been there just under two years, and a round of severe budget cuts meant that his position was eliminated. I was staying home with our twin boys, who were two years old at the time, and so I had no income. This situation sent both of us into a panic. What would we do? How would we survive? We had children to take care of, mortgage payments on our brand new house. I couldn't see past the debilitating fear that we would not recover from this blow. I couldn't trust that God was a part of this new turn our lives had taken. I felt that God was very far away indeed. Well, it turned out that God didn't really need my trust. He was there anyway, just as He *always* is. My husband went on a string of interviews, and by August had secured a new teaching position in a great school district only fifteen minutes from our house.

Mark was lucky to find a job pretty quickly. It could have just as easily taken him much longer, and things could have gotten a lot tougher for us. It's only looking back that I can see that one way or another, we would have been ok. The story ended the way it was going to end. The only variable was how much time I spent worrying about it. And isn't that really all we can control in this world...our approach to the storms that we face? Aman. To be certain of God's faithfulness. This kind of belief provides us tremendous comfort as we move through life. God will never abandon us. God will always keep His promises. We may not always know *how* He'll do it—which can be very scary for people used to being in control of our lives—but we know that He will.

In fact, I propose that believing in the unfailing faithfulness of our God is our only job. All goodness, joy, and meaning stem from this unshakable belief. Even during the darkest times, when you are paralyzed with fear, worry, or suffering...this is precisely the time to lift your eyes to the Lord, who made heaven and earth. To stand firm in the knowledge that God's love and faithfulness will never change. Believe this even during those periods of darkness, when it seems like we have absolutely no contact with God. God wants us to trust Him completely, especially when there is silence and darkness.

And again, I completely acknowledge that it's a very hard thing to do. But God doesn't expect us to do it alone. He gave us the gift of Jesus—our Cornerstone.

So this is what the Sovereign Lord says: "See, I lay a stone in Zion, a tested stone, a precious cornerstone for a sure foundation; the one who relies on it will never be stricken with panic."

ISAIAH 28:16

Jesus is the foundation upon which our faith rests. Those who believe and build their lives around this Cornerstone will stand firm through the trials of life. This rock is what will help us withstand anything that life brings. We can make it through the hard times, because we know God will be with us every step of the way, and he gave us His only Son to prove it.

QUESTIONS FOR REFLECTION

1. When do you find it the most challenging to place your trust in God? Think of people you know who seems to have complete and unfailing trust in God. Ask them to share their secret!

2. Spend some time in the days to come thinking about Jesus as our Cornerstone. How does that affect your worries and fears?

A Foundation of Faith

I walked into my bedroom one day to find my husband teaching our boys how to tie a tie. We didn't have any special occasions coming up so I asked him what prompted this. "They'll be leaving for college soon," he answered. "I only have five more months to teach them grownup stuff." Later that week he took them outside to show them how to jump start a car.

I understood what he was doing. He wanted to give them a foundation before they left us. To make sure they had what they needed to launch into adulthood and live on their own. It's the same reason my dad taught me how to balance a checkbook, and my mom taught me how to cook before I left for college.

It got me thinking about my own foundations—figurative and literal. My dad is a homebuilder, and when I was a little girl, he would take me and my sisters to new developments where basement foundations had been poured and dried, ready for the framing of a new house. These lots became our playground. Holding tightly to my dad's hand, we used to run across the hardened concrete like a wide balance beam. The foundation was strong and sturdy. We knew it would hold us up.

That's what our faith does for us. It holds us up. It's solid and steady and helps us feel safe and grounded when the winds blow and the rains lash. Jesus beautifully illustrated this during his Sermon on the Mount:

> *"Therefore everyone who hears these words of mine and puts them into practice is like a wise man who built his house on the rock. The rain came down, the streams rose, and the winds blew and beat against that house; yet it did not fall, because it had its foundation on the rock. But everyone who hears these words of mine and does not put them into practice is like a foolish man who built his house on sand. The rain came down, the streams rose, and the winds blew and beat against that house, and it fell with a great crash."*
>
> MATTHEW 7:24-27

In many ways, our faith is something we have to initiate. We have to "practice our faith" or "believe." And because of this, we may find that our relationship with God swells and dips, and sparkles and fades over the years. But there's another way to look at it. Our gift of faith is in fact initiated by God, our loving Creator. Just like parents doing their best to provide their children with the tools they need to succeed in life, God has provided us with everything we need. The foundation of God's love, strength, and power is always there. Steady and strong...like a rock. "The Lord is my rock, my fortress, and my deliverer" (Psalm 18:2).

All we really have to do is what Jesus teaches us: "Listen to these words of mine and act on them." And keep clinging to the Rock of Ages, no matter what.

PART FIVE:

GOD'S LOVE

We love because He first loved us.

1 JOHN 4:19

Come As You Are

A few years ago my husband and I spent an amazing week on a tropical island in the Caribbean. The weeks leading up to the vacation were stressful for me. I was tired from work, pale and washed out from the long winter. I was fighting a cold, and my lower back had a consistent ache from sitting for long hours at work. Worst of all, I had not reached my ideal weight for wearing a bathing suit. I was putting so much pressure on myself to "fix" all of these things before we left. This was a trip of a lifetime, and I wanted everything to be perfect.

Seeing how anxious I was, my husband said: "Isn't the point of the vacation to rest and heal and relax?" The thought hadn't occurred to me, and his words calmed me down right away. I didn't need to be perfect before I arrived. I could come to our vacation exactly how I was. Let the sun, the ocean, and the tropical air work its magic on me.

Come as you are.

This is God's invitation to us—to know us and be in relationship with us just as we are. Wounds, regrets, scars, bruises, and doubts...God wants all of it. We don't have to do any frantic preparation in order to make ourselves "ready" for God. We just need to show up. All I needed to do to enjoy the healing benefits of that tropical vacation was to get on the plane. In the words of C.S. Lewis, "God doesn't want something from us, He simply wants us."

You don't have to be perfect before you come to God. You are made perfect in God's love. You don't need to fix yourself so that God will accept you. Bring your deepest wounds to God, and let the healing begin. You don't need to rest up so you'll have the energy to be what God wants you to be. You can find rest—and profound peace—in God.

In words attributed to Abigail Van Buren, "The church is not a museum of saints, but a hospital for sinners." Whatever your experience of faith or worship is, think of the doors to a church as a metaphor for your relationship with God at this moment. Where do you find yourself? Outside the closed door...afraid to open it and come in? Or maybe standing in the open doorway...peering inside, wondering if there's a place for you?

You don't have to be a "saint" or saintly to live a life of faith. Very few people are! In my experience, so many of us hold ourselves back from a truly authentic relationship with God because we feel inadequate or "not enough." In her book *Days of Deepening Friendship*, Vinita Hampton Wright writes:

> *"No matter what state you're in when you enter the Room, it has no impact whatsoever on God's love for you. God's invitation is sweet and clear: Come in! There is so much to know and to experience. And you will be astounded by the divine moment called love."*

Our faithful God provides all the love, healing, and rest we could ever need. All we need to do is show up.

After a week of lying on the beach, sleeping late, and feeling the warmth of the sun—I was transformed. My cold faded away, my skin lost its winter pallor, my aching back was healed from long soaks in the hot tub and a massage. (I confess I didn't make any progress on reaching my ideal weight...all-inclusive buffets are really, really tempting!) The healing and restoration my husband promised me would happen, happened that week. I simply needed to trust that it would.

My prayer for you today is that you will trust in the faithfulness of our loving God. Trust that God will welcome you with open arms. Come as you are and accept God's invitation. Open the door and come inside. Just simply show up, and let God take care of the rest.

Broken and Beautiful

A few years ago, a very dear friend showed me a page from her journal. It was a letter she had written. "Dear God," it read. "Please help me fix the following things about myself." And it went on for two pages, listing 20 or 30 things she felt were wrong about her. It broke my heart. If only she could see what I saw. A devoted friend, wife, and mother. A funny, warm, enthusiastic person who cared so much about others. I wanted to shout at her, *"Rip up that list!"*

Like so many of us, my friend saw herself as something broken. A cracked pot not worthy to be displayed on a shelf of precious objects. But what I saw in my friend was longing. A longing to be better. To become some perfect ideal of herself, before she felt truly loved and accepted by God. Waiting until she was whole.

What I've come to realize since then is that this kind of waiting is not the answer. Our cracks are part of who we are. But more than that, they're actually critical to a deepening relationship with God. We need our cracks. We need our brokenness. Playwright Heather McDonald wrote one of the most beautiful lines I have ever read in all of literature:

"It is said that grace enters the soul through a wound."

What if we stopped looking at our cracks as barriers to God, but instead saw them as openings through which God's love and grace might enter our souls? In the story of Creation, Adam and Eve needed to experience original sin and be expelled from the Garden of Eden, so that we all might experience the gift of salvation. This fall from grace—this first and ancient wound that we all carry inside of us—brought about the most beautiful act of sacrifice the world has ever known.

Greek mythology gives us a story about a curious young woman named Pandora who opened a box. Out of the box escaped all the evils of the world. This is how the ancient Greeks tried to make sense of a world full of brokenness. But according to the myth, at the very bottom of the box, there lay hope. We experience this same phenomenon today. We must live through the ugliness of despair, in order to

76

appreciate the beauty of hope. The COVID-19 pandemic and the racial justice protests of 2020 brought about acts of caring and devotion from healthcare workers and activists that were truly beautiful to witness, even in the midst of so much turmoil and division. We can find signs of hope amidst so much brokenness.

Yet another way to illustrate this idea of God's grace entering our souls through our brokenness can be found in a Robert Frost poem called "Mending Wall." You may be familiar with this poem...it's the one that contains the well-known line: "good fences make good neighbors." In the poem, two neighbors get together every spring to mend the cracks in the wall that separates their property. A common interpretation of the poem is that the barrier between them is what allows them to maintain a cordial relationship. But a closer look reveals just the opposite. It's the time they spend together mending the wall that sustains the friendship. The cracks and broken places in the wall provide the opportunity for a richer relationship. And so it can be with each and every one of us as we strive for a deeper closeness with God.

What these stories reveal to me is that we don't have to wait until we're completely whole to have a relationship with God. God wants us to come to Him just the way we are...cracks and all. In fact, there's a particular beauty in our brokenness. After all, it was the broken body of Jesus—beaten, whipped, and nailed to a tree—that brought us the ultimate salvation. We celebrate this every week at Eucharist in the breaking of the bread. The crucifixion is the ultimate proof that God doesn't shy away from brokenness.

God's sending Jesus to suffer and die a brutal death was an act of profound love. Do you believe it? Can you believe that God loves you that much? In Isaiah, the Lord says to us:

I have called you by name. You are mine. (Isaiah 43:1)
I have engraved you on the palms of my hands.
(Isaiah 49:16)

John 3:16 says: "For God loved the world so much that he gave his one and only Son, so that everyone who believes in him will not perish but have eternal life." We are God's beloved. Take a moment to really reflect on the enormity of that statement. You are God's beloved.

Can you fathom such a love? Can you fully comprehend the impact this Divine love can have on the way you see yourself and the way you live your life? One thing I know is that God's love has never been dependent on our being perfect. When Jesus lived on earth, he spent his time with the poor, the meek, the sick, and the sinful. None of these could claim to be perfect. Yet Jesus loved them. Just as Jesus loves us. Not because we're perfect...but because we belong to God.

My prayer for you today is that you will begin to look at your cracks as sacred opportunities to experience God's amazing love. Spend some time with Jesus at the Mending Wall. Give your flaws over to God, and let His grace enter through every wound.

QUESTIONS FOR REFLECTION

1. Can you think of a time when you held yourself back from God because of your flaws or imperfections? How did this "holding back" manifest itself in your life? (Did you stop going to church? Did your prayer life suffer? Did you cut yourself off from people that you loved?)

2. What might it feel like to let God's grace enter your soul through your wounds? How do you imagine God might react to those wounds?

The Voice of Truth vs. the Inner Critic

I'd like to introduce you to someone. Someone you're all too familiar with because he or she is with you all the time. It's your Inner Critic. We all have one. Some are louder than others. And some are meaner than others. The Inner Critic is that voice inside your head that only has negative things to say. That tells you that you don't look beautiful. You're not smart enough or talented enough. It's the voice that constantly compares you to your friends, coworkers, and teammates, and insists that they are better than you. The Inner Critic judges your body, your intelligence, your beauty, and your talents.

I'm not talking about the voice that challenges you to work hard, set goals, and make good choices. That's the Inner Coach in you (otherwise known as your conscience), and she's healthy and helpful and necessary. The Inner Critic is much more damaging, and the things she says are *not* true.

The worst part is, you can't escape the Inner Critic, because he's inside your head. She's loud and constant, and you can't turn her off. He's always there to drown out anything positive you may think or feel about yourself, or anything positive you may hear from others.

Now you might ask, what's so harmful about an Inner Critic? Doesn't it keep us from being arrogant or overconfident? Doesn't it challenge us to be better or try harder? In truth, the Inner Critic does no such thing! It leads you to feel worthless, undeserving and small. If you exclusively listen to the voice of your Inner Critic you'll withdraw and hide away. You'll deprive the world of the wonder that is YOU!

If your friend talked about herself the way your Inner Critic talks about you, you would want to put a stop to it. You wouldn't want your friend to believe those things about herself. So why should you believe such things about *yourself?*

I'd like to take you back to the moment of your creation. We know from Scripture that we are created by God in God's image. St. Paul writes: "we are God's masterpiece"—God's greatest piece of work (Ephesians 2:10). Each of us was created by God to be a unique masterpiece. How would God look upon His own work? Would He call it names? Would He criticize it? Would He be ashamed of it?

Instead of focusing on the voice of your inner critic, I encourage you to listen for the Voice of Truth—the voice of your loving God. The voice that says you are loved and accepted exactly the way you are! You are *never* alone. God is by your side all the time. He knows and understands you. God notices you and cares about you, no matter how trivial you think your life might be. You are God's Beloved Child and He loves every part of you...even the parts you think are the most unlovable.

That's the Voice of Truth...and it's the only voice that matters.

In My Father's Eyes

What are some motivations that you may need to confess?

This was the question posed by my writing prompt one winter morning, and it immediately made me think of the past Thanksgiving. After starting a new health regime in September, I had lost a bit of weight. I was feeling pretty good about myself and bought a new outfit to wear for Thanksgiving dinner at my parents' house. I played the scene out in my head. I would enter the house, take off my coat, and everyone would be amazed at how great I looked. I would be showered with compliments and admiration. It was going to be a great holiday.

Imagine my surprise when no one seemed to notice at all.

It was a humbling lesson in pride and vanity. If I had kept my focus on either the real meaning of Thanksgiving—being thankful for my loved ones and all our blessings—or the true benefits of losing weight— improved long term health—I would have felt incredibly blessed that day instead of vaguely disappointed.

I won't beat myself up about it. It's perfectly human to want praise and compliments. I don't believe it's a sin to want people to think well of you. But it's a slippery slope when it comes to motivation. In the wise words of Ron Swanson from *Parks and Recreation*: "Don't start chasing applause and acclaim. That way lies madness."

When I first started giving spiritual retreats, I was desperate for positive affirmation. Like Sally Field at the Oscar's *("They like me! They really like me!")*, I drank up praise like it was the most addictive drug on the market. I told myself it was affirmation from God I was searching for. If people kept telling me how good I was, then I knew that was what God wanted me to be doing.

I'm not sure how sound my reasoning was. The truth was, I just liked the feeling.

Again, it wasn't the worst thing in the world to enjoy some praise, as long as I didn't lose sight of the reasons I was doing this in the first place. My desire to please God by helping others had to outweigh my desire to please *myself* by helping others. It's a fine line of distinction, but it feels important.

It's a good idea once in a while to examine why we do the things we do. Are there motives that are preventing us from living in a real and authentic way? Is it more important for me to get a hundred "likes" on a blog post than to reach one person who really needs to hear God's message, even if I never know about it? Social media leads us down this path to "madness" like nothing else. It's all about the numbers. Followers...hits...page views...likes...friends...retweets. Many people long to be "famous" or "popular" in whatever platform they can. For the most part, this can be harmless fun (and I'm not suggesting that everyone uses social media in this way!), but chasing applause is a race we'll never win, because we'll always want more. If we measure our success by the numbers, we'll always be left feeling dissatisfied.

What do you place at your center? Validation from outside forces? Or the love and adoration of God, who created you? "The LORD does not look at the things people look at. People look at the outward appearance, but the LORD looks at the heart" (I Samuel 16:7b). I can think of no better audience that that, and God is always going to be our biggest fan. The One who knows us best. The One who sees us for who we are and still loves us.

QUESTIONS FOR REFLECTION

1. What are some motivations that you may need to confess?

2. What do you place at your center?

God Smooths Out Our Jagged Edges

Have you ever taken a close look at a river rock? These flat rocks, found in riverbeds and on beaches, are unique in size, shape, and color but with one similarity. They are smooth. No jagged edges, sharp corners, or pointy bumps.

What makes these rocks so smooth?

Water flowing in a river is constantly moving. A powerful force that carries along dirt, sediment, and smaller stones in its path. These rough items bump up against the rocks, acting like sandpaper. They break off the pointy bumps, round out the sharp corners, and smooth the jagged edges. This is a natural process, called weathering or erosion, that occurs over a long period of time. The end result is a smooth and shiny stone, beautiful in its purity.

Can we compare this process to our own lives?

At times, are you the jagged rock? Uneven and rough. Covered in sharp edges that cause pain in your own life or the lives of those around you. Each rough spot representing a heavy burden, a sharp tongue, a harsh response, a jealous thought, or a past pain. Without realizing it, you become something that causes others to wince upon contact. Something that cannot hold or be held.

Or do you feel like that rock being tumbled around in a swirling river? Bumped and tossed. Crashing into those around you—or being crashed—with a force you feel you can't control. It can make you feel helpless...or even hopeless. There's no gaining your footing in such a riotous atmosphere.

I encourage you to look at this in another way. The pain is real, but the process is powerful and profound. The driving force is the water, and it's no random occurrence. The water represents the Divine Source that is constantly washing over your jagged soul, breaking off those burdens and pains. Carrying them away. Smoothing them out.

We believe in a loving God that shapes us in this way. We are first introduced to this Living Water at our Baptism. An outward sign of an inward grace. A never ending flow of mercy, love, compassion, and forgiveness. The process isn't always easy. Weathering can be painful! Life tosses us around whether we like it or not. God uses these "tossed" experiences to shape us. God uses our trials to smooth us out until we are transformed. "See, I am doing a new thing!" (Isaiah 43:19)

All you have to do is let it happen. God is always working in you, whether you realize it or not. Let the healing water of God's love rush past you and surround you, making you smooth, shiny, and new.

If you'd like to become more tuned in to the ways in which God is working in you, try prayer, meditation, or reading and reflecting on the Word of God. You'll find yourself gaining in awareness of God's constant and overflowing presence in your life.

May God bless your journey and continue to polish you into a shining reflection of His love.

QUESTIONS FOR REFLECTION

1. At your next opportunity, take a look at a smooth stone. (You can Google a picture if you don't have easy access to a river or beach!) As you gaze at the surface, use God's eyes to search for your shining reflection. What do you see?

2. Do you see the grace-filled moments of your life reflected back at you? Can you see the unfolding of your purpose? Can you see God's promise and His deep love for you?

Part Six:

Letting Go

All that God asks you most
pressingly is to go out of yourself –
and let God be God in you.

Meister Eckhart

Let it Go!

During a few blustery, rainy days here in New England, I watched the autumn leaves fall like snow. (Reminding us of what was to come!) My imagination conjured the sad image of the trees desperately clinging to their many-colored coats as they struggled to hold on against the unrelenting wind. A few days later, after reading a scientific article, I was surprised to learn what was really going on.

In autumn, trees "decide" to let go of their leaves.

In the warm and fruitful days of spring and summer, leaves use sunlight and water to make food for the tree. With the coming of winter, these leaves become inefficient and unable to produce food. In order to survive the harsh winter and allow for new growth in the spring, a deciduous tree must shed its leaves and seal off the spots where they were growing.

This is done through a process called abscission. When the Northern days grow shorter and colder, trees release a hormone that causes tiny cells to grow at the spot where the leaf stem meets the branch. These are called "abscission" cells. (Think "scissors.") These cells form a line that weakens the leaf stem and allows the wind to do the rest.

A very different metaphor then what I originally imagined. A story of struggle and loss gives way to one of empowerment and growth. Instead of holding on in vain, the trees are actively participating in a process of letting go. What a powerful example of how we might choose to live! Think of the autumn leaves as habits, behaviors, or ways of thinking that are no longer life-giving or sustaining. By letting go of them, we—like the trees—allow for protection, preparation, and new growth.

And so I ask...is there something you need to let go of?

What are you holding onto that prevents you from growing? Perhaps it's an old hurt that has festered in you. Or wounding messages from the past that shape the way you view yourself. Maybe it's a toxic relationship that is tearing you down instead of building you up. Just like the autumn trees, you can *decide* to let go of the resentment, bitterness, self-judgment, or critical thinking.

Or maybe instead of holding on, you've been holding back. What are you clinging to that might block you from moving forward? Fear? Doubt? The desire to stay with what's safe? Maybe it's time to let go of that fear and try something new. Does the thought of doing this scare you? That's ok. Change is always scary. These views, habits, or hurts have been a part of us for so long, that releasing them can almost feel like a small death. We're afraid we might not recognize ourselves anymore. But remember, the process is part of a necessary cycle. Just as the trees are preparing for the long, cold winter, sometimes in order to protect ourselves, we need to let go. To release. To unclench our fists and allow the cycle of dying and rising. This will make way for something new...surprise, wonder, and awe.

If you're still fearful, the good news is that you're not in this alone. Not even close! Remember, leaf-shedding is a two-part process. The tree does its part, and the *wind* comes along to do the rest. Think of that wind as the Holy Spirit dwelling within you. Allow yourself—through God's grace—to embrace abundance and joy. If there's something in your life that needs shedding, imagine God whispering to you: *"Let go...let go."* Make the decision to release it, and allow God to carry it away with the wind.

> *Forget the former things;*
> *do not dwell on the past.*
> *See, I am doing a new thing!*
> *Now it springs up; do you not perceive it?*
> *I am making a way in the wilderness*
> *and streams in the wasteland.*
>
> (ISAIAH 43:18-19)

One thing we know from watching the endless turn of the seasons...winter may be long and brutal, but springtime *always* comes. A resurrection bringing new life and new growth. The practice of letting go is a cycle we can participate in over and over again throughout our lives. If at first we don't succeed, we can always try again. As St. Paul said in his letter to the Philippians:

> *I don't mean to say that I am perfect. I haven't learned all I should even yet, but I keep working toward that day when I will finally be all that Christ saved me for and wants me to be. No, dear brothers, I am still not all I should be, but I am bringing all my energies to bear on this one thing: Forgetting the past and looking forward to what lies ahead.*
>
> PHILIPPIANS 3:12-13

QUESTIONS FOR REFLECTION

1. Have you become entrenched in ways of thinking that are not life-giving or sustaining? Are you "stuck" in unhealthy ways of relating to others?

2. How might God's love enable you to LET GO, so that you might be filled with new energy and life?

Leaving Our Nets Behind

As Jesus was walking beside the Sea of Galilee, he saw two brothers, Simon called Peter and his brother Andrew. They were casting a net into the lake, for they were fishermen. "Come, follow me," Jesus said, "and I will send you out to fish for people." At once they left their nets and followed him. Going on from there, he saw two other brothers, James son of Zebedee and his brother John. They were in a boat with their father Zebedee, preparing their nets. Jesus called them, and immediately they left the boat and their father and followed him.

MATTHEW 4:18-22

In Matthew's Gospel we hear the beautiful story of Jesus calling two sets of brothers, Simon and Andrew and James and John, to drop their fishing nets and follow Him. This reading is one of the gospel stories I remember most distinctly from my childhood. Not just because I liked the story—although I did enjoy it—but because something about it made me supremely uncomfortable. It always boggled my mind how quickly those men dropped everything to follow Jesus. Matthew uses the phrases "immediately" and "at once," suggesting that the brothers didn't stop to think about it for even a moment.

As a kid, I wasn't prone to doing anything spontaneously, preferring to think things through before making my move. And so I marveled at how these brothers were able to do this. I often wondered...what else did they leave behind? Their mothers? Sisters? Were they married? Did they have other commitments? If they weren't fishing, who was providing food for their families? All of these musings really pointed to the one question I couldn't bring myself to ask—the question that was at the root of my discomfort with this story:

If I was one of those fishermen, and Jesus called me to follow him, would I drop everything "at once" and go? There was a part of me that always wondered if perhaps I wouldn't be able to do it. That I just didn't have it in me.

Have you ever felt the same way? That you might be one of those people clinging to your fishing nets, unable to let them go and follow Jesus. What holds us back? What are the nets that we've become tangled up in...that tie us down and prevent us from being free to follow Jesus? It's important to reflect on this question, for if we can't identify these nets, we can never be free of them.

I believe the answer can be found not in where we cast our nets, but in where we cast our eyes. Imagine for a moment, you are standing on the shore. The air smells of sun and dampness, a warm breeze flits across your skin as you drag your net along the water's edge. Jesus approaches you and says, in a quiet yet compelling voice, "Come along with me."

Where do you direct your gaze when Jesus speaks to you? Are your eyes cast downward, unable to look directly at His face? Do you feel too ashamed or too unworthy to look Him in the eye? I believe this feeling of unworthiness can be the single biggest impediment to living a life with meaning. And it's absolutely without foundation. God loves us and accepts us exactly the way we are. Psalm 4:1a says, "O God, you have declared me perfect in your eyes." Does this mean we're perfect? Of course not! Only God is perfect. So what does this line from Scripture mean? Years ago I attended an evening retreat where the presenter said the following: "God has a plan and a purpose for you, and He made you exactly the way He needs to you to be." You can disagree with that statement, feeling you have far too many flaws for God to ever want to use you for much of anything—but you'd be wrong.

Ralph Waldo Emerson once wrote, "What is a weed? A plant whose virtues have not yet been discovered." You may think of yourself as a useless weed, unworthy when you compare yourself to the beautiful flowers around you, but God knows who you truly are, and what you can accomplish, if you would simply drop your net and follow Him.

O Lord...you made all the delicate, inner parts of my body, and knit them together in my mother's womb. Thank you for making me so wonderfully complex! It

is amazing to think about. Your workmanship is
marvelous – and how well I know it.

If God made each and every one of us so wonderfully unique and flawed and complex, why wouldn't He want to use us for an important purpose? I believe if you stood on that seashore and told Jesus you couldn't follow Him because you weren't good enough, He would laugh gently and say, *"Silly child, my Father made you this way for a purpose. Come... let's see what you can do."*

QUESTIONS FOR REFLECTION

1. What holds you back from following Jesus? What nets are you clinging to?

2. How easy is it for you to believe that God has a plan and purpose for your life, and that God made you exactly the way He needs you to be?

Finding Purpose in the Journey

How often do you find yourself asking the age-old question: What is my purpose in life? We know that God is calling us, just like Jesus called the disciples to come and follow Him, but how do we know what God is calling us to do? Where's the roadmap...or the specific set of instructions?

I should be honest and say I don't really have an answer to this question. But I do have a theory. For some reason, God doesn't choose to reveal Himself to individuals in the same way. I believe those people who hear a more distinct calling—like the 12 disciples—are quite rare.

For reasons beyond our understanding, God wants the rest of us to embark on our journeys without really knowing where we're headed. In many ways, this "not knowing" becomes the greatest stretch of our faith. There's a plaque that used to hang in my old office with the following quote by Martin Luther King, Jr.: "Faith is taking the first step, even when you don't see the whole staircase." What better way to show our trust in God than to set out on this blind journey, confident that He will reveal Himself to us when the time is right? That God will reveal our purpose when we're ready to hear it? So for those of you who come up blank when you ask yourself, what is my purpose in life...it's ok. Maybe you're not supposed to know what your purpose is just yet. Maybe it's enough to say you'll know it when you see it.

So...what do we do in the meantime?

To quote a popular phrase, "Keep on keepin' on!" Just because God has chosen not to reveal His plans for you just yet, that's no reason to go running back to the security of your fishing nets. For now, let the journey become your purpose. Let the journey become your calling. Commit yourself to leaving the seashore and following Jesus, wherever He might lead you. Commit yourself to taking the next step on the staircase. To the belief that Jesus is leading you to your destiny.

The next time you see a spider web, think about—comparatively speaking—how far that spider had to travel to complete the web. If you stretched all the tiny little lines and squares of the web out into a straight line, imagine how long it would be! But a spider doesn't travel in a straight line. I read this in a book, once, and it really stuck with me: to make a web, a spider must continually return to a center point. Like a compass that always points North, this constant return to center is what enables the spider to create that intricate and beautiful spiral shape we are so familiar with.

So a spider is really taking a series of little journeys, always coming back to center. I challenge and encourage you to do the same. Keep your relationship with God at the center, and venture out on an endless series of little journeys...with each one, learning more about yourself and more about your purpose in life. This allows you to keep moving, even when you don't have all the answers. And I absolutely believe that's the way God wants it. He wants us to venture out on the journey without knowing exactly where it will lead. He wants us to be open to it. He wants us to learn, to make mistakes along the way, to keep on keepin' on. And this becomes so much easier to do when you know you can always come back to the center—to God.

The only thing that God does NOT want is for us to give up the journey entirely. For it's what happens on this journey that will give our lives purpose.

REFLECTION ACTIVITY

Sketch a picture of a spider web on a blank sheet of paper. Use the spaces between the web to reflect on some of the "little journeys" of your life. How can you keep God at the center? Think of times you have been successful at doing that, and times when you did not feel God's presence in your journey.

Praying to be Disturbed

Do you have the same habits that guide your spiritual life throughout the year? The same weekly prayer service, the same bedtime prayers, the same religious practices. Although there's something very comforting about routines and rituals, they can also turn into a kind of "spiritual inertia," and it can be a powerful experience to shake off that inertia and allow ourselves to be disturbed.

What does it mean...to be disturbed? It's a word that has a pretty negative connotation, doesn't it? When something is disturbing, it's usually not good.

Not necessarily.

Picture the way a strong wind disturbs the branches of a tree, moving them and shaking them a little. Now imagine that wind is the Holy Spirit blowing through your soul. How is it moving you? In what ways is it stirring up your faith? Let yourself embrace this feeling instead of avoiding it. This is called "Holy Disturbance." It prevents us from playing it safe or phoning it in.

I once heard someone refer to this feeling in way that spoke to me: "God is trying to ruffle my feathers," she said. She knew that God was calling her to do something different. She wasn't quite sure what it was, but she sensed she needed to be open to it.

My birthday is in December, and a few years ago it fell on a Sunday. I announced to my husband that the only thing I wanted to do for my birthday was stay in my pajamas all day, curl up on the couch, and watch the latest *Avengers* movie. My husband went a bit pale because unbeknownst to me, he had arranged for all of our friends to join us with their families for a massive traveling scavenger hunt, looking for various Christmas related items. (You had to find and take pictures of things like a carton of eggnog, a Santa on a rooftop, a decorated mailbox, an outdoor nativity scene, etc.)

I had to very quickly shift gears. Instead of my relaxing day on the couch, I would go on an exciting, breakneck journey through the

94

neighboring towns, ending with a rowdy and fun lunch at a local restaurant. Not at all how I expected my day to go, but so much more fun and meaningful than what I had planned for myself.

At the post-scavenger lunch one of my dear friends asked me if I wanted to join her for an Advent candlelight labyrinth walk later that evening. Now, if she had called me when I was in the middle of watching *The Avengers*, I can guarantee I would have said no. I would have been firmly rooted to my couch with no desire to go anywhere. But the scavenger hunt had already "disturbed" my plans and opened my heart to this spirit of adventure. So I said "yes," and my birthday ended with an incredibly moving, peaceful, and faith-filled walk through a silent labyrinth experience.

Spend some time thinking about how you react to change. Do you welcome it, or do you shy away from it? What if you began to look at change as God calling you? A calling that stirs your heart and moves you to a deeper level of faith. How often do you say "yes" to those opportunities? If you feel like you've gotten into a rut in your spiritual life, I offer you this old anonymous prayer to reflect on.

> *Disturb me, Lord, when my dreams come true, only because I dreamed too small. Disturb me when I arrive safely, only because I sailed too close to the shore. Disturb me when the things I have gained cause me to lose my thirst for more of You. Disturb me when I have acquired success, only to lose my desire for excellence. Disturb me when I give up too soon and settle too far short of the goals you have set for my life. Amen.*

ANONYMOUS

PART SEVEN:

EVERYDAY SPIRITUALITY

There is a time for everything, and a season
for every activity under the heavens.

ECCLESIASTES 3:1

Finding God in the Pots and Pans

I wonder if, like me, you've ever felt like there were two people inside of you. There's the "busy self" who does all the everyday stuff: working, shopping, running errands, cooking, cleaning, paying the bills, taking care of everyone...and the "quiet self" or some might call the "holy self" who is focused on quiet prayer, listening to God in the stillness, going on retreats—all those great things we're encouraged to do but never seem to find the time for. And so we struggle with this feeling that when we're dwelling in the "busy self" we're not quite "holy." We're not measuring up to the ideal.

Well, I don't believe God wants us to live in this fractured or compartmentalized way—when we're praying, we're praying, but when we're working, we're working. It doesn't have to be that way. It's entirely possible to encounter God, or spend time with Jesus, amidst the hustle and bustle of all we have to do. In the words of St. Theresa of Avila..."God is in the pots and pans."

As you go through the mundane tasks of an ordinary day, it's hard to imagine God hanging around. This is pretty boring stuff! As you sit pouring over your tax return, it's hard to imagine God sitting there with you. God is about prayer and connection. Not money and math. As you stand at the sink washing dishes, it's hard to imagine God standing with you. This chore is absolutely void of any divine spark. Or is it?

Brother Lawrence, a 17th century monk, was devoted to this teaching of St. Theresa of Avila and he promoted a form of spirituality called *The Practice of the Presence of God.* He came up with this when he was assigned to the monastery kitchen, where he spent all day cooking and cleaning for his superiors. He found this common kitchen work to be an ideal place to discover and feel God's presence. He writes:

> *"Men invent means and methods of coming at God's love, they learn rules and set up devices to remind them of that love, and it seems like a world of trouble to bring oneself into the consciousness of God's presence. Yet it*

might be so simple. Is it not quicker and easier just to do our common business wholly for the love of him?"

This is a beautiful and appealing idea to me. The fact that our kitchens (or any place, really) can become a chapel, where God is wholly present. This chapel can be our office, our car, our backyard...wherever it is that we find ourselves conducting the busy chores of our day. When we invite God into our workspace, whatever routine thing we're doing is immediately elevated to the holy. Because God is there, and God loves us, and we can feel God's presence with us at all times.

For Brother Lawrence, there was no fractured self. He found a way to be his "holy self" no matter what he was doing. And those mundane chores? God cares about all of them! You don't have to worry about God being too bored, too busy, too specialized, or too lofty. God cares about every little thing you do. All you have to do is remember to invite Him along. Don't put Him off, saying: "I'll get to my prayers as soon as I'm done with this list," or "I'll spend quiet time with Jesus when I get the chance." Remember, Jesus was called Emmanuel..."God is with us." Whatever you're doing, invite God in. It just might transform the experience for you.

QUESTIONS FOR REFLECTION

1. Are there times when you feel a conflict between your "busy self" and your "holy self"? How is your relationship with God affected by this conflict?

2. Do you believe that God cares about your average, everyday work and daily family life? What do you think Jesus might say to you about the work that you do?

Pray Where You Are

For many years I've been collecting a book series on spirituality called *Elf-Help Books* by Abbey Press. The series contains over forty mini-books on a variety of topics, each one accompanied by charming illustrations of elves drawn by R.W. Alley. Titles include *Trust-in-God Therapy, Stress Therapy, Forgiveness Therapy, Keep Life Simple Therapy, Be-Good-To-Your-Marriage Therapy,* and many more. The books are beautiful in their simplicity; 35 to 40 short statements to help you reflect on each topic.

One of my favorites is *Prayer Therapy,* written by Keith McClellan, O.S.B. In the foreword he writes:

> *Real prayer is organic—it grows out of your own life, personality, needs, and rhythms. Each day and every moment are filled with opportunities for prayer. If we seize these moments, we open ourselves to the greatest enrichment—and most effective therapy—possible. Prayer isn't for specialists. Prayer is for you and for me.*

I love this idea that we all have access to a rich prayer life if we only embrace it. Prayer is not reserved for only the most holy. It does not take place only in churches. It does not have to consist of poetic words. Prayer is simply a connection to God in whatever form that may take for each one of us. As Fr. McClellan suggests: "Pray where you are. God is everywhere." In line at the grocery store. In classrooms. On a busy street. Deep in the woods. High on the mountaintop. In the depths of the valley.

You can bring any emotion or thought to prayer. God loves you and knows you best, and He wants to hear it all! Bring your gratitude to God. Your sorrow. Your anger. Your confusion. There may be times when you can't even find words for what you're feeling. Let your sigh become a prayer. Or your tears. Or a shrug of your shoulders. Or a clenched and shaken fist. God knows what your heart is experiencing and is listening and loving you.

If you pray where you are often enough, you'll find it becomes a part of you. A "second-nature" response to every situation. This living, ongoing conversation with God will enrich your life in countless ways. Answers will come. Peace will come. Contentment will remain.

Fr. McClellan closes his book with this beautiful thought: "To pray is to breathe. Do it deeply and you will be filled with life." Amen!

QUESTIONS FOR REFLECTION

1. Are you able to "pray where you are?" What are some of your favorite places for praying?

2. Do you ever pray without words? What do those prayers from your heart look like?

Called to Holiness

When you think of a "holy" person, what image comes to mind? Perhaps you think of your pastor, a nun, or some other member of the clergy. Or that person in your parish who attends daily Mass. Or the volunteer who devotes his or her time to soup kitchens, food pantries, and other charitable organizations.

When you imagine a holy person...do you ever picture yourself?

To be holy is to be like God. Doesn't that seem kind of lofty? *How on earth could ordinary ol' me achieve such a thing?* The answer lies right in the question. Holiness doesn't come from the "earthly" world. It's not something we earn, or work towards, or deserve. It's a gift from God. As St. Paul writes in his letter to the Ephesians, "God chose us in him before the creation of the world to be holy and blameless in his sight" (Ephesians 1:4).

God *chose* us. How beautiful!

So what exactly does it mean to be holy? Many saints and Christian authors have written about this topic. For today, I look to three Theresas to shed light on this topic:

- "Holiness is a matter of bringing our wills into union with God's will" (St. Theresa of Avila).

- "Holiness consists simply in doing God's will, and being just what God wants us to be" (Thérèse de Lisieux).

- "Holiness does not consist in doing extraordinary things. It consists in accepting, with a smile, what Jesus sends us. It consists in accepting and following the will of God" (Mother Theresa).

The gift of holiness comes to us in the journey, as we follow God's will and try our best to live as God would have us live. In doing so, we become the best version of ourselves. Pope Francis spoke beautifully about this topic in a Vatican Radio address in November 2014. "To be holy is to rediscover ourselves in communion with God."

For me, the best part about holiness is that it's a universal call. We are *all* called to be holy. It's not a special status reserved only for the most pious. So even on those awful days when you're stressed out, grouchy, and at odds with the world, if you bring those feelings to God and ask Him to work in you...you are holy. If you keep God at the center of all you do...you are holy.

It encourages me to realize that holiness can be lived out in the most ordinary tasks. I don't have to escape to a cloistered mountaintop and live my days in silence in order to answer the call to holiness. I can be holy while making dinner for my family. Or answering phone calls at work. Or shopping for groceries. As Pope Francis went on to say:

> *"This is it: every state of life leads to holiness, always! At home, on the streets, at work, at church, in the moment and with the state of life that you have, a door is opened on the road to sainthood. Do not be discouraged to travel this road. God gives you the grace to do so. And this is all that the Lord asks, is that we are in communion with Him and serve others."*
>
> POPE FRANCIS, NOVEMBER 2014

QUESTIONS FOR REFLECTION

1. Spend some time thinking about the gift of holiness that you have received from God. What does that gift look like in your life? In what ways has that gift transformed your heart?

2. In what ways can you "rediscover" yourself on the road to sainthood?

Let God Shine Through You

John the Baptist had no problems being the "guy behind the guy."

In the region of Judea—where Jesus was baptizing people—John was nearby, also performing baptisms. John's followers began to worry that Jesus' ministry was starting to eclipse John's. They approached John with concern, jealousy and maybe a little resentment. "Master, the man you met on the other side of the Jordan River—the one you said was the Messiah—he is baptizing too, and everybody is going over there instead of coming here to us" (John 3:26).

John reminds his disciples that he is not the One. "You yourselves know how plainly I told you that I am not the Messiah. I am here to prepare the way for him—that is all" (John 3:28). He compares himself to the best man at a wedding, waiting for the groom to arrive, and rejoicing when he does. And then he speaks these beautifully humble words about Jesus: "He must become greater. I must become less" (John 3:30).

John knew his ministry wasn't to testify to his own greatness or his special role in the story of redemption. It was to introduce Jesus. To step aside and let the story continue. John was there to be a witness to Christ. How can we live out these words of John the Baptist and follow his example in letting God become greater in our lives? What does this "becoming less" look like in our daily lives?

STEP ONE: BELIEVE IN GOD'S LOVE

Truly believe that God loves you and has a plan for your life. This is where you must begin, for if you can't see God at work in your life, you'll be stuck in a world of self-doubt and ego-driven insecurity. Wake up every morning saying, "I was created to be loved by God." This is the profound truth that grounds us in all that we do...the stunning reminder that we are loved unconditionally by God.

STEP TWO: EMPTY YOURSELF

John the Baptist's disciples were caught up in feelings of envy and arrogance. This focus blocked them from recognizing the truth that John was there to testify. When we allow ourselves to be filled up with negative attitudes that don't serve us, we leave little room for Jesus. If we empty ourselves of self-serving junk—insecurity, envy, selfishness—we create space for Jesus to enter and dwell in our hearts.

STEP THREE: PRACTICE GRATITUDE

The act of becoming less doesn't mean denying the core of who you are, or downplaying your gifts or talents. Quite the opposite! Recognize that everything wonderful about you came from your Creator. Every time you feel good about something you did or accomplished, take a moment to thank God for making you exactly the way that you are.

STEP FOUR: LET GOD SHINE THROUGH YOU

Be the "guy behind the guy." Let God shine through you. Each day, carefully examine your words, your actions, and your motivations to make sure they reflect God's love. Instead of focusing on your own goals for the day, focus on your interactions with others. Make it your mission to let others see in you the shining reflection of Christ's light.

As Paul writes in his letter to the Corinthians: "We are therefore Christ's ambassadors" (2 Corinthians 5:20). Keep God at the center of all you do. Seek out the good for others before your own. Invite Jesus into all your daily interactions and see how the experience is transformed.

When Re-Gifting is OK

Be honest, have you ever re-gifted something? Not your proudest moment, was it? That's ok, we've all done it. It's your child's final violin lesson of the year and you forgot to pick up a thank you gift for her teacher. Desperately searching the house, you find a vanilla-scented candle that your neighbor gave you last Christmas. It's in perfect condition. You never got around to lighting it. So you throw it into a recycled gift bag from Mother's Day with some tissue paper from your most recent purchase at Macy's. Your daughter is good to go and hopefully her teacher will be none the wiser.

This kind of last-minute gift scramble is something we feel sheepish about and would never admit to. It somehow diminishes both the giver and the receiver, not to mention the original giver!

Believe it or not, there are times when re-gifting is not only acceptable but encouraged. We receive tremendous gifts from God, our Creator, and He wants nothing more than for us to give them away.

LOVE

Jesus gives us a great commandment: "Love one another as I have loved you" (John 15:12). We are meant to take the gift of God's love and use it as an example of how we are to love and treat others. Jesus taught us how to do this in his every action. He humbly washed the feet of his disciples. He loved the sinner, the leper, and the outcast. He loved us to the point of death on a cross. How far are we willing to go to share His gift? Do we love those who challenge us? Do we love those that the world rejects? Do we love those who believe they are unlovable?

FORGIVENESS

Jesus teaches us about the amazing gift of God's forgiveness through parables like the Prodigal Son (Luke 15:11-32). Surely this lost son might have received a blistering lecture from his father when he returned home. At the very least a resounding "I told you so!" Can we be inspired by this prodigal forgiveness to re-gift it upon those who hurt us? Have you been clinging to anger towards someone because of stubbornness or pride? Can you follow God's example and forgive?

GRACE

When my grandmother turned 80 years old, we had a big party for her and she received many gifts. As she opened each one she exclaimed, "I don't deserve this!" This sweet declaration of feeling is the best way of describing grace; simply put, "the unmerited favor of God towards humankind." Abundant blessings pour over us no matter what we do or how we behave. This undeserved gift is incredibly humbling and not to be taken lightly. St. Paul tells us that we are "faithful stewards of God's grace" (1 Peter 4:10). I try to remember this when I'm tempted to snap at my husband or criticize my children. Is there a more grace-filled way to interact with them? Am I truly living my life as an instrument of God's amazing grace?

My prayer for you today is that you will be aware of God's amazing gifts and be on the lookout for opportunities to re-gift them to the world.

A Look Beneath the Surface

The window in my office looked out over a pretty little tree that bloomed with beautiful pink flowers in the springtime. It brightened my day all season to look out on this splash of color. One day I happened to look up from my computer to the shocking sight of this tree slowly and quietly falling to the ground. Huh? What happened! It wasn't stormy or even windy out. What knocked this tree over?

I went out for a closer look and realized that half of the tree was badly diseased. Some kind of white fungus or mold had killed off the leaves and weakened the branches. I was heartbroken to realize that the tree had been slowly dying and I never even noticed. I walked by that tree every single day on my way into work, but only appreciated it for what it could give me, a pretty view during the spring season.

How often do we do that with the people in our lives—look only at the surface? The brave face they are presenting to the world? But if we looked a little deeper, we might see sadness, pain, or worry. Obvious sorrow is easy to see and respond to. But quiet suffering takes place under the surface. The only way to discover it is by taking a closer look. Paying attention to those around us. Shifting the focus from our own lives for a little while to listen and be present to others.

Jesus was good at noticing those who were lost, dejected, and silently suffering.

In Luke's Gospel we learn of a woman who had been bleeding for twelve years and could not be healed. When Jesus passed by, she came up behind Him and touched the edge of his cloak. Jesus asked His disciples who had touched Him and they shrugged it off, assuming it was just the crowd pressing in on Him. Not satisfied with that explanation, Jesus took the time for a closer look. As He searched the crowd, the woman came up to Him and fell at His feet. By her faith she was immediately healed (Luke 8:43-48). The Gospels are full of stories like this. Jesus was all about connection and healing. He wanted to reach everyone.

I'll never know if there's anything that might have saved that tree. But if I had been paying better attention, I could have called the groundskeeper. He would have diagnosed the tree and possibly even healed it. It was a sad lesson to learn and one that has inspired me to be more present to those around me. To focus less on me and more on others. A reminder that everyone I meet is a child of God. Everyone is worth a closer look. I pray to follow the example of Jesus as I strive to look beneath the surface. To listen and really hear. And to serve.

Seeing With Eyes of Faith

One morning while driving to work, I put on my sunglasses and quickly realized that they were smudged, making everything a bit blurry and unfocused. I could see well enough to drive safely, but I couldn't wait for the next red light so I could clean them. Wouldn't you know...for the first time in the history of my commute, I hit nothing but green lights all the way! So I was stuck with a smudgy view for this ride.

It took an embarrassingly long time for me to realize the solution was simple—just take off my sunglasses. Ah! My vision cleared and everything looked crisp and bright and focused. The experience got me thinking about "vision" and how we see the world. It reminded me of a gospel story we hear during the season of Lent.

Meet Bartimaeus, a blind beggar who lived on the streets of Jericho. Life was difficult for Bartimaeus, but his blindness and his life on the streets made him adept at hearing and listening. He had heard stories of a man they called Jesus who could heal people with the touch of His hand. A man who told stories about lost sheep, a mustard seed, and a new kind of kingdom where all were welcome at God's table. Bartimaeus knew if he could just meet this amazing man, maybe touch His cloak, perhaps he, too, could be healed (Mark 10:46-52).

It was this rock-solid faith of a blind beggar that drew the attention of Jesus on the road to Jericho. Instructing His disciples to bring the man to Him, he asked Bartimaeus what it was that he wanted.

"Son of David, I want to see."

Seven simple words and his life was changed forever.

"Go," said Jesus, "your faith has healed you."

Though he was blind, Bartimaeus did not lack vision. He was able to "see" with eyes of faith. He could see—and believe—that Jesus came to bring us new life and a new way of living. He believed that Jesus was here to show us the way if we only seek Him.

Let's take an honest look at how we view the world. Are there times that we see through the smudged glasses of fear, jealousy, anger, or indifference? Are we unable to see what's really going on because of entrenched ways of thinking? Does ignorance make us blind to the suffering of others or the true feelings of others? When we fail to see with eyes of faith, our world is smudged, like my cloudy commute to work. We can't see what's really important.

We aren't blocking out the "sun" with these glasses. We're blocking out the Son.

Let us pray that Jesus, the healer, will open our eyes and help us let go of whatever it is that prevents us from seeing things clearly.

QUESTIONS FOR REFLECTION

1. What are the things that tend to cloud your vision, making it difficult to see God more clearly?

2. If you removed your "smudged sunglasses," what do you think you might see?

A Time to Speak

There is a time for everything, and a season for every
activity under the heavens...
A time to be silent, and a time to speak

ECCLESIASTES 3:1,7

As a young girl I was shy and deeply introverted. This resulted in a rock wall of silence that took me years to chip away. In my high school classrooms I never spoke. I answered every question in my head. I came up with witty responses to the silly banter of adolescence, but never actually delivered them. My teachers begged me to participate, but the words just wouldn't come out. Looking back at my high school yearbook, I notice how many notes from teachers and acquaintances remarked on how quiet I was. Only to my friends did I open up and reveal my inner life. I felt safe with them. I could trust them with my truth.

This reticence lessened in college and more so in graduate school, but only by a little. My graduate advisor understood. She knew I wasn't just sitting there, disengaged with all that was happening in class. In fact I was quite busy. I was learning, discovering, uncovering, soaking in, turning over, deciding, proving, agreeing, dissenting. All this was happening within the safe walls of my own mind. I knew that more was expected of me, but the words just wouldn't come out. Almost like a crowd of people trying to get out of an elevator all at once. They were wedged in. Stuck. If you're an introvert like me, this feeling is probably all too familiar.

One day in a private meeting in her office, my advisor said to me: "Sometimes, the person who says nothing can be the most active participant in the class. Dynamic listening is a gift. But someday you're going to have to share what's going on in there."

It took a degree of bravery that I did not find until I was almost forty years old. Like the Sara Bareilles song:

Say what you wanna say
And let the words fall out
Honestly—I wanna see you be brave

When I started giving retreats, speaking out about God's love and God's presence in our lives, I had finally found my voice. It was only through prayer and the gentle gift of God's guidance that I felt brave enough to put my thoughts on paper and speak them aloud. Just like that beautiful line from Ecclesiastes, I had come into my season to speak.

Towards what season is God guiding *you?*

Do you have a gift or talent that you're keeping hidden or silent? Can you hear God whispering to you, asking you to share that gift? It requires a degree of bravery, but remember, God gives us all the strength and courage we need. "A city located on top of a hill cannot be hidden, nor do they light a lamp and place it under a basket, but on a lampstand, and it shines on all those in the house" (Matthew 5:14-15).

At my first retreat presentation, I stood in front of a crowd of 60 women, wide-eyed and expectant. I wasn't afraid. It didn't occur to me that my ninth-grade self would have shriveled and hid at such a scene.

I got up...and the words fell out.

Live Like You Were Living

I have a confession to make. I am not a fan of the songs, inspirational quotes, and Facebook posts that tell us to "live like you were dying." I get the point. Time is short. You have to make the most of every moment. You never know when your number may be called. My reaction to this: It's a terribly nerve-wracking way to live your life! This pressure to do everything we think we might ever want to do for every moment of the day. To tell everyone exactly how much they mean to us every single time we interact with them. I think if I tried to live this way, I would fall asleep each night convinced I had fallen woefully short of the demands of this "live like you were dying" philosophy.

For example, here are some things I did today: I cleaned my bathroom. I wrote a few emails. I made a grocery list. I stared into space for a few minutes while trying to focus on work. I spent a few minutes trading dumb jokes and harmless gossip with my sister. I watched TV.

Not exactly skydiving and poetry.

The fact is, most of us live pretty ordinary lives. It's how we choose to frame that "ordinary" that matters. And we don't need a death knell to achieve it. We just need a simple reminder that God loves us. That God is good. And that God chooses us and blesses us. The process of becoming who we're meant to be is often gradual. We are each a work in progress. We look back on the ordinary moments and realize that our life is about something...or it is not yet. But there's still time. For the vast majority of us, there's still time to make changes.

I'm not rejecting bold action in living out our faith. There will be those times when God calls us to take risks. To abruptly change course. To follow Him in a direction we never dreamed we could go. But most days we're just chugging along the tracks of life. Doing our best. Imagine if every time you did something, a voice shouted at you: *"But you could DIE tomorrow! Is that really what you want to be doing on your last day on earth?"* My goodness. Who could hold up under that pressure? Imagine instead, that you heard a voice whispering to you:

"You are loved. You are called to love."

This gentle reminder would reshape the way we see the world. The way we interact with others. The way we live.

There are many ways to live life to the fullest. And it's true that some of our loved ones have been taken from this earth far too soon, while still others face very serious medical struggles. Our heart breaks with the unfairness of it all. We may never understand the reasons for it, and we wish we could take their place. But we must remember that God has given us our time here on earth for living. It's ok to have regrets...as long as we share those regrets with God, release them, and keep moving forward, through each ordinary moment, listening for God's voice teaching us and reminding us that love matters most of all.

It just might be a feeling even better than skydiving.

Part Eight:

An Allegory of Five Gardens

It is like a mustard seed, which a man
took and planted in his garden. It grew
and became a tree, and the birds
perched in its branches.

Luke 13:19

Allegory of Five Gardens (Part One)

Long ago, in a land far away, there lived five sisters. The Master Gardener, who loved them all very much, gave each sister a gift—a small plot of land to plant a garden. With excitement and hope, they prepared the soil and planted seeds, giving them lots of water and sunshine until they sprouted into healthy plants. As time went on, the five sisters tended to their gardens in their own different ways.

Months later, the Master Gardener invited each sister, one at a time, to come and share with him how her garden fared. The first sister approached with hesitant steps and slumped shoulders. She could barely look the Master Gardener in the eye.

"How does your garden fare, my child?"

"Not well, I'm ashamed to say. My garden is dry as dust. All the plants have withered and dried up, and the soil is hard and cracked."

"Do you know why?" the Master Gardener asked with gentle but questioning eyes.

"Lack of water, I suppose," she answered with a sigh.

"My dear one, you know that I have an abundant source of flowing water. You need only have asked, and I would have given you all the water you desired. Why did you never come to me?"

The sister paused before answering. "Lots of reasons, I guess. Sometimes I was just too busy. It seemed like the distance was too far to travel to get to the water. Other times I felt too unworthy to ask you for such a precious gift. After a while, I no longer remembered the water you had to offer."

With a nod of understanding, the Master Gardener sent a steady rainfall to drench and quench her garden and bring it back to life. The plants and flowers responded immediately. The roots were strengthened, the leaves returned to bright and vibrant shades of green.

Flowers opened as the stems stretched tall to absorb the warm sunlight that followed the rain.

Tears of gratitude filled the eyes of the first sister, and she promised him she would never again forget about this precious gift that was hers for the taking.

REFLECTION

Does your faith life ever resemble the dried up and withered garden of the first sister in this story? You're stuck in a rut, uninspired, and unable to access the powerful connection you once felt to God—The Master Gardener. You feel more distant from God than ever before, unable to hear His whispers or feel His presence. Your faith life feels lifeless.

You are not alone. We all go through spiritual dry spells from time to time. Some ending quickly, others stretching out for a much longer time. God has given each of us our own personal Garden of Eden, lush and beautiful and overflowing with the abundant blessing of God's love for us. But like any garden, it needs nourishment. God gives us the Living Water of Jesus Christ to nourish our spirit and bring us to new life.

Being in a spiritually dry place is not always a bad thing. God may be preparing us for something or reminding us of our dependence on His gift of grace. We need to live through the dry time in order to more fully engage in the fruitful spirituality that is to follow.

What's important is to recognize those times when we are depleted or dry, for they can sneak up on us. "O God, my God! How I search for you! How I thirst for you in this parched and weary land where there is no water. How I long to find you!" (Psalm 63:1) The next time you find yourself in the dry garden of faith, let your prayer become a conversation with God.

Dear Lord, my spiritual garden has become dried up and wilted. Why do I feel this distance? What is getting in the way of a closer intimacy with You? In Your wisdom, reveal to me the path that has led me to this place of thirst and dust. Remind me of Your gift of grace, that I may seek life-giving water and come alive again.

Find a quiet place to spend some time alone with God. Pray for inspiration and ideas to reconnect with God in a personal way. Read Scripture, attend a retreat, or talk to a friend. Be gentle with yourself and have faith that this season of dryness will pass. Remember, even the most dead-looking plant is often only dormant, waiting for the first light of spring to come to life again.

Allegory of Five Gardens (Part Two)

Long ago, in a land far away, there lived five sisters. The Master Gardener, who loved them as his own, gave each sister a gift—a small plot of land to plant a garden.

Months later, the Master Gardener invited each sister, one at a time, to come and share with him how her garden fared. The second sister approached with dragging steps and slumped shoulders. Her cheeks were reddened from hours in the sun, and her tired eyes revealed dark smudges underneath.

"How does your garden fare, my child?"

"Too well, I'm afraid to say. I wanted to plant as many things as I could, to thank you and praise you for this wonderful gift. So I have perennials and annuals, creeping plants and climbing plants, vegetables and fruits. The garden is truly bursting with life."

"Then why do you look so unhappy?" the Master Gardener asked with kind but questioning eyes.

"Now it keeps me so busy I'm exhausted all the time. There's so much work involved. Weeding, pruning, watering. It never ends. It's gotten to the point where I don't even enjoy working in my garden anymore."

"My dear child," the Master Gardener replied. "I gave you this gift so you could find joy in your work. An overcrowded garden will not thrive, and it will only leave you feeling tired and cross. You need balance and simplicity."

The Master Gardener helped her cut out sections of her garden (to pass along to other members of the village) and install a bench, where she could sit and rest in the shade and enjoy the beautiful bounty of her smaller and simpler garden.

A sigh of relief escaped her lips as the second sister delighted in the extra time she had to spend in quiet solitude. She promised never again to take on so much work that she forgot the reason she planted in the first place.

REFLECTION

Does your faith life resemble the overcrowded garden of the second sister? You're involved in everything. You're part of every church committee, prayer group, ministry, and Bible study. You can't say no to anything. Like the sister Martha from Luke's gospel, you're overwhelmed with all the work you have to do.

This is a common situation for people who are actively involved in ministry and volunteer work. It's called "church burnout," and many of us are all too familiar with this feeling. Our busy schedule of church commitments begins to wear us down. It becomes a chore and even builds resentment. "Why do I have to do everything!"

Serving God through church ministries shouldn't come at the expense of spending time with God. The church work you do shouldn't become a block to deepening your relationship with God. Some points to consider:

EXAMINE YOUR MOTIVES

Why do you feel compelled to do so much? Is it an attempt to prove yourself worthy to God? A desire to impress others in the church? An inability to say "no"? There's no doubt that God wants us to serve others. We see that in the example of his son, Jesus Christ. But we also see moments when Jesus left the crowds to go off by Himself, taking time for quiet prayer and solitude. Look for this same kind of balance in your own faith life.

SET REALISTIC BOUNDARIES.

Once you become identified as the "go to" volunteer for getting things done, you'll find you get called on for lots more. Be prepared for this, and learn to say no if the work is getting to be too much.

TAKE A BREAK

"Come to me all you who are weary and burdened, and I will give you rest" (Matthew 11:28). God's grace is not dependent on a numbered list of good deeds we've accomplished. You'll be no less deserving of that grace if you scale back a bit. Remember, God want us to live healthy, balanced lives. The garden of your faith life should reflect that.

So if you're feeling like this second sister, take some time to sit in your garden and pray. Block out all distractions of fundraisers, committee meetings, and potlucks. Come to God in the silence and rest in His loving embrace. You'll be glad you did, and your faith garden will find new life after a period of rest.

Allegory of Five Gardens (Part Three)

Long ago, in a land far away, there lived five sisters. The Master Gardener, who provided all that they needed, gave each sister a gift—a small plot of land to plant a garden.

Months later, the Master Gardener invited each sister, one at a time, to come and share with him how her garden fared. The third sister approached with shrugged shoulders and confusion in her eyes.

"How does your garden fare, my child?"

"Not well, and I don't understand why! I sit in my garden every day and pray. For hours I offer prayers of thanksgiving and praise. Yet my garden is a mess! Weeds are sprouting up everywhere, crowding the healthy plants and robbing them of sunlight and nutrients."

"My beloved daughter," the Master Gardener replied. "Your prayers are always welcome, but I gave you this garden as a gift, in the hopes that you would care for it through your actions, not just your prayers. The garden needs you if it's going to thrive. You must show your love by tending it."

Understanding dawned on the third sister's face as she realized what she had failed to do. Running home, she spent an entire day cleaning up her garden. Pulling weeds, pruning, watering, and feeding her plants. As a result, it flourished. She had healthy, nutritious vegetables to feed the poor and hungry in the village. She promised never again to forget to do her part.

REFLECTION

Jesus came to preach a radical message of love and social justice. Our actions matter just as much as our words. Piety and prayer—while extremely important—are not enough. Jesus challenges us to feed the hungry, give drink to the thirsty, welcome the stranger, clothe the naked, care for the sick, and visit those in prison. He reminds us: "whatever you did for one of the least of these brothers and sisters of mine, you did for me" (Matthew 25:40).

Introverts like myself are very good at finding time for quiet prayer, but more challenged by the idea of living our faith through action—or interaction in this case. God's gift of grace is ours for the taking, but we must be active participants in this gift. We do so by living out Jesus' message of love. By becoming the face and hands of Jesus for all those we encounter. In the parable of the Good Samaritan, it is the Samaritan—not known for being pious or obedient to the law—who wins the praise of Jesus through his act of compassion. So many of Jesus' parables emphasize the importance of putting our faith into action through our deeds.

A faith lived in words only will resemble the neglected garden of the third sister. Take some time this week to look for ways in which you might reach out to others to spread Jesus' message of love. Come up with an "action plan" for the rest of the month or the next season. You will be rewarded with a garden filled with abundant love and grace as you begin to fulfill God's purpose and plan for your life.

Allegory of Five Gardens (Part Four)

Long ago, in a land far away, there lived five sisters. The Master Gardener, who loved them all very much, gave each sister a gift—a small plot of land to plant a garden.

Months later, the Master Gardener invited each sister, one at a time, to come and share with him how her garden fared. The fourth sister marched right up with her head held high and a satisfied smile on her face.

"How does your garden fare, my child?"

"Oh, you have to come see it!" she exclaimed. "I threw away the seeds you gave me because I knew they wouldn't produce the biggest, most colorful blooms. The flowers I chose are amazing! The prettiest in the village. Every day I stand outside so I can see the villagers walk by my garden and marvel at how beautiful it is."

"My beloved daughter," the Master Gardener replied. "While it is true I gave you the garden to do with as you pleased, it seems as if your only goal is praise and admiration. Your garden can be used for so much more. To grow food for the poor. To provide a quiet place where you might sit and pray. You have turned it into nothing more than a showpiece."

The fourth sister was humbled by the words of the Master Gardener, and she realized he was right. It had become too important to her to have the biggest, most beautiful garden. From that day on she replaced some of the more ostentatious blooms with beans, peppers, and tomatoes, which she shared with all who were hungry. And in the early morning, when no one else was around, she spent time reflecting and praying in her garden. Over time, it came to mean so much more to her than the dazzling display she used to show off to the village.

REFLECTION

If we take an honest look at ourselves, I'm sure there are times we've been guilty of behaving like this fourth sister. Putting on a show

126

of our faith. Praying to impress. We may not even realize we're doing it. It's perfectly human to want people to think well of us, but it shouldn't take the place of an honest and intimate relationship with our loving Father. In Matthew's gospel, Jesus says:

> *And when you pray, do not be like the hypocrites, for they love to pray standing in the synagogues and on the street corners to be seen by others. Truly I tell you, they have received their reward in full. But when you pray, go into your room, close the door and pray to your Father, who is unseen. Then your Father, who sees what is done in secret, will reward you.*

MATTHEW 6:5-6

A common misinterpretation of this Gospel passage is that Jesus is condemning public prayer. But we know this is not the case. When Jesus takes the seven loaves and fishes, he breaks the bread and very publicly gives thanks to God before sharing the food. This is what we do every Sunday when we gather to worship. Praying in community is not what Jesus calls into question here. Instead, Jesus challenges us to examine our motives.

Ask yourself these questions:

1. Am I praying to put on a show, to garner praise from others, or to compete?

2. Is it more important for me to be seen as pious and spiritual than to really be present to God while I am praying?

3. Am I making my prayer life all about me instead of all about God?

Years ago I belonged to a prayer group that gathered together once a week to pray for our children. I often received praise for the prayers I offered, compliments on a particular turn of phrase or the words I chose. I liked the feeling so much that the weekly sessions became like a performance for me. I was determined to impress each week with my prayers. In my efforts to earn praise and compliments, I began to lose sight of why I was praying in the first place. It was a humbling lesson to learn.

Prayer life isn't about appearance. It should go much deeper than that. Prayer is conversation with God—words we speak to our loving Father directly from our hearts. We don't need an audience or a stamp of approval from our peers to achieve this kind of close relationship with God. Let your garden of faith become a time of quiet stillness. A time of praying and listening.

Allegory of Five Gardens (Part Five)

Long ago, in a land far away, there lived five sisters. The Master Gardener, who loved them all very much, gave each sister a gift—a small plot of land to plant a garden.

Months later, the Master Gardener invited each sister, one at a time, to come and share with him how her garden fared. But the fifth sister did not appear. After waiting for some time, the Master Gardener went out in search of her, and found her sitting in her cottage, staring blankly at the walls.

"I've come to ask about your garden," he said. "How does it fare?"

"I have no idea. I prepared the soil and planted the seeds like you asked me to. And then I built a high stone wall around it to protect it from the rabbits and deer."

"Tell me what grows in your garden?" the Master Gardener gently pressed.

"I really don't know. I haven't been in there in months. I just don't see myself as a gardener. There are days I think about going inside, but it's been so long now, that I don't know what I would do in there."

"My beloved daughter, I gave you this garden as a safe and sacred space. It is yours. All I ask is that you enter and sit awhile."

The fifth sister did as the Master Gardener asked. She sat in her garden for a morning...and felt nothing. She returned for the next three mornings, and still nothing. On the fifth morning, she sat quietly in her garden and felt the sun warming her face. She watched a butterfly dance among the flowers. She breathed in the scent of earth and nectar and rain. She was overcome with a rush of feeling. A memory of the love she felt on the day she received this precious plot of land. Peace settled deep within. She vowed never again to wall herself off from her garden.

REFLECTION

A life of faith isn't always easy. We wrestle with questions, doubts, and disagreements—matters that must be explored through deep prayer and examination of conscience. The process can be daunting. We witness those who claim to be Christian, yet do and say things that contradict the loving message of Jesus Christ. We see people use the name of Jesus to hurt and reject others. We don't want to throw ourselves in with that lot. We don't want to be anywhere near them. So we distance ourselves from the Church. It may seem easier to close ourselves off from the more challenging aspects of our faith. Avoidance is always easier.

Though our doubts may be justified, it's our response to these doubts that can often drive a wedge between us and God's love for us. But walling ourselves off from the love of God isn't the answer. And the longer we do this, the more our faith becomes a remote and distant memory. Bring your questions to God. Bring your doubts, your anger, your dissonance. Trust that God loves you and will help you work through this time of uncertainty.

Just like the fifth sister, God only asks that you enter the garden and sit with Him for a while.

PART NINE:

SEASONAL REFLECTIONS: ADVENT AND CHRISTMAS

For unto us a child is born,
unto us a son is given.

ISAIAH 9:6

Making Room for Jesus

*And she gave birth to her first child, a son. She wrapped
him in a blanket and laid him in a manger, because there
was no room for them in the village inn.*

LUKE 2:7

On the night our Savior came into the world, there was no room
for him. I can only imagine how Mary and Joseph must have felt. Tired
and dusty from the long trip through Galilee and Judea. Mary, heavy
with child, uncomfortable, frightened, knowing with a woman's
intuition that her time was near. Joseph, realizing with dread that they
would not make it home in time, and their child would have to be born
here, in Bethlehem. This brave couple, so very young and alone,
desperately searching for a safe place to give birth, only to be told there
was no room at the local inn.

John the Baptist says, "The Kingdom of Heaven is near...Prepare
the way of the Lord!" Just like that innkeeper in Bethlehem, during this
holy season of Advent, we are being asked to make room for Jesus in
our lives, in our hearts, and in the world.

How will we respond to this request?

If Jesus were literally coming to stay in a room in your house, how
would you get that room ready for Him? Over the years, my guest room
has become the catch-all place for storing junk. It would take a mighty
effort to prepare it for a Divine guest. Clearing away piles of old school
papers, out-of-date magazines, and outgrown clothes. Giving it a
thorough dusting and vacuuming. Putting crisp, clean linens on the bed.
Adding some touches of beauty, like fresh flowers or a nice-smelling
candle. I'm not sure how long this would take, but I have a feeling Jesus
would be waiting a while!

Having a cluttered and chaotic room like this is kind of a burden.
A friend of mine who works with computers once used the following
analogy to explain why computers start to operate more slowly over

time. Imagine if every time you walked through a room you put down a box filled with papers. Eventually, the boxes would become so cluttered and piled up, that it would take you a long time to navigate the room. That's why computers act sluggish when the disk space is filled up.

And so, during this Advent season, I invite you to do some spiritual housekeeping. What are the boxes that are cluttering up your heart, making it difficult for God's love to navigate? What is the disk space you need to clean out? Perhaps there's that box labeled "stress" crammed with demanding schedules and never-ending to-do lists. Or some files filled with the clamor and noise of relentless social media. Maybe another box contains regret over past mistakes or anger over old hurts.

Whatever your personal "clutter" may be, cleaning up is easier than you think. Give every one of those boxes to God! He's waiting to shoulder the weight.

> *Come to me, all you that are weary and are carrying heavy burdens, and I will give you rest. Take my yoke upon you, and learn from me; for I am gentle and humble in heart, and you will find rest for your souls. For my yoke is easy, and my burden is light.*
>
> MATTHEW 11:28-30

Let this Advent season be a time of awareness. Discover the presence of God in all that you do and all that you see. God is everywhere! Look for Him in everything! Clear out the "room" of your heart so it is prepared to receive the overwhelming, awesome, life-changing gift of Jesus Christ. Allow the Prince of Peace to fill you up in a totally new way.

Come, Lord Jesus!

Mary's Yes

True confession time. For most of my life I did not pray to Mary. I wasn't in the habit of saying the Rosary. And I did not have any statues of the Blessed Mother in my home or garden. Mary had always seemed a lofty ideal to me. A heavenly image of perfection that I could not live up to or relate to. I once heard a priest say that our Church hadn't done Mary any favors by putting her up on a pedestal. The higher she was raised up, the more remote she became.

Years ago, a friend recommended that I read a book called *Two From Galilee* by Marjorie Holmes, a dramatic account of Mary's story—a teenage girl chosen by God to bring Christ into our earthly world. The Mary depicted in this story was one I found infinitely compelling: young, scared, and facing an overwhelming responsibility. Discovering Mary through the prayer of imagination was the moment she became real to me.

Who was Mary? What was her life like? What was the historical context in which she lived? Only by learning Mary's personal story can we find our own story. And the Advent season is where Mary's story begins.

> *In the sixth month of Elizabeth's pregnancy, God sent the angel Gabriel to Nazareth, a town in Galilee, to a virgin pledged to be married to a man named Joseph, a descendant of David. The virgin's name was Mary. The angel went to her and said, "Greetings, you who are highly favored! The Lord is with you."*

> *Mary was greatly troubled at his words and wondered what kind of greeting this might be. But the angel said to her, "Do not be afraid, Mary; you have found favor with God. You will conceive and give birth to a son, and you are to call him Jesus. He will be great and will be called the Son of the Most High. The Lord God will give him the throne of his father David, and he will reign over Jacob's descendants forever; his kingdom will never end."*

"How will this be," Mary asked the angel, "since I am a virgin?"

The angel answered, "The Holy Spirit will come on you, and the power of the Most High will overshadow you. So the holy one to be born will be called the Son of God. Even Elizabeth your relative is going to have a child in her old age, and she who was said to be unable to conceive is in her sixth month. For no word from God will ever fail."

"I am the Lord's servant," Mary answered. "May your word to me be fulfilled." Then the angel left her.

LUKE 1:26-38

What a powerful story! God chooses Mary and comes to her with an invitation. Mary's response to this invitation is life-changing and world-changing. What did it take for Mary to say "yes" to God? For "Pedestal Mary"—all divine perfection and poised serenity—it probably wouldn't be that difficult. But the Mary we meet in Scripture wasn't on a pedestal. She was fully human, a young woman "greatly troubled" by this encounter with God's messenger. I have been blessed with a very rich imagination, but even I have trouble visualizing what this must have been like for Mary. We know that Mary had great faith and love for God, but how did she feel in that moment? Shocked? Afraid? Confused? Or a glimmer of something bigger?

Despite this probable whirlwind of emotions, Mary responds, "May your word to me be fulfilled." What characteristics did Mary possess that made God choose her and allowed her to say yes? She was open to God. She was willing to put her trust in Him and to give up her own plans. In Mary—in this moment—we see a complete surrender to God's will.

During the Advent season we are encouraged to lay our story down next to Mary's. Just like this young maid of Nazareth so many years ago, God chooses us and comes to us with an invitation. How will we respond? Are we open to the mystery of God's plans for our lives? Can we follow Mary's example and take a leap of faith?

On October 13, 2013, Pope Francis celebrated Mass in St Peter's square in honor of the Marian Day and had the following to say about Mary's example to all of us:

> *"Today let us all ask ourselves whether we are afraid of what God might ask, or of what he does ask. Do I let myself be surprised by God, as Mary was, or do I remain caught up in my own safety zone: in forms of material, intellectual or ideological security, taking refuge in my own projects and plans? Do I truly let God into my life? How do I answer him?"*

Mary was asked to bring Christ into the world. As Christians, we are asked to do that very same thing. Not in the same way that Mary was, but in the way we live our lives. In the way we interact with others. In the words we speak. In the deeds we do.

Do our lives diminish Christ or bring him forth?

Taking Jesus to the Mall

It's that season again. When countless sermons and blog posts deliver the same message: we're doing Christmas all wrong. We're focusing on the trappings and the noise instead of the true meaning of Christmas. Through all the gift giving and party planning, we're forgetting whose birthday it really is. The stress of planning and decorating is distracting us from what's really important.

My reaction to these statements...*they are not helpful at all!*

This commentary (for you can't even really call it advice) is not rooted in a woman's reality. We can't abandon these things, because it's our job. There's a quote you've probably heard by British poet Arthur O'Shaughnessy: "We are the music makers, we are the dreamers of dreams." (You may remember Willy Wonka saying this line in the movie *Charlie and the Chocolate Factory*.) Well, as women, we are the Christmas makers and we are the creators of Christmas dreams. Our job is making memories...and it's an incredibly valuable one.

And so telling us that the things we're rushing around doing is making us forget the true meaning of Christmas is only going to make us feel guilty and conflicted. It creates that fractured self I've written about earlier in this book. There's the "busy self" who does all the shopping, baking, gift wrapping etc. and the "quiet self" or some might call the "holy self" who is focused on quiet prayer, waiting in the stillness...all those great things we're encouraged to do during Advent but never seem to find the time for. And so we struggle with this feeling that when we are dwelling in the "busy self," we're not quite holy. We're not measuring up to the ideal of the season.

I don't believe God wants us to experience Advent in this fractured way. And I don't believe it's necessary. It is entirely possible to wait for Jesus amidst the hustle and bustle of the holiday season. We're not losing the true meaning of Christmas amidst the shopping, planning, cooking, and visiting...in fact, we're living it.

The way we do this is by bringing Jesus along with us, and keeping Him the focus of all that we do during this busy, hectic, noisy, festive, special, loving season.

Jesus can be a part of our festivities and our planning every step of the way. You can continue to see Christ in all that you do this season. Every twinkly light hanging from every tree in every store of the mall represents Jesus. Because Jesus is Light. The light in the darkness that will lead our way to the Promised Land. That is something to be celebrated, whether it's done through a beautifully carved nativity set in a stately church or through a handful of tinsel on a gaudy tree.

Remember, we do what we do out of love...and Jesus *is* love. So if you're excited to take Jesus along with you this season, here are some practical examples of what you can do:

- When you're at a party, take a moment to look around, and imagine Jesus there. What would He be doing? Who would He be talking to? What might He be saying? Remind yourself that Jesus Christ dwells within each and every person at that party...even those people you find particularly challenging.

- When you're at the shopping mall standing in a long line, take a moment to say a loving prayer for each person in line ahead of you. Ask Jesus to bless them, to grant them a peace-filled holiday season, and to touch their lives in some small way this Advent season.

- When you're baking cookies or wrapping gifts, say a prayer for the recipient of the gift. Ask Jesus to bless the gift and the person who will receive it.

I'm not suggesting you abandon all attempts for quiet reflection during Advent. It's incredibly enriching, so savor those moments when you can! But I also encourage you to look for any opportunity to take Jesus along with you as you get ready for Christmas this year.

An Introvert's Guide to Advent

My sister and I have a long-standing joke that she's my "Wake Wingman." I'm an introvert and so immersing myself in large crowds has never been my thing. Small talk can be draining for me. I also internalize emotions and wakes are brimming with feelings. My sister, on the other hand, is a gregarious, extroverted, social being. She always knows what to say, and large crowds of overflowing emotion bring out the best in her. So whenever possible, I tag along behind her at wakes. I mean, I literally stand behind her the whole time, glued to her side. As we work our way through the line, she says something to the neighbor or co-worker, and I nod my head in agreement, offering a sympathetic look or a gentle smile if appropriate. We've been doing this for years, and it works for us. My expression of sorrow is no less sincere; it just has a different delivery method.

It got me thinking about the challenge for introverts to live out the message of Jesus. Jesus was all about relationships. Love your neighbor, help the poor, gather in communities to pray. For some, this comes as naturally as breathing. Serving a meal to a hundred patrons of a soup kitchen would leave an extrovert feeling energized and ready to take on the world. For introverts, we would want to crawl under the covers and turn out the lights. Not because we don't love our neighbors. Or we don't care about helping those in need. It's just harder for us. Being an introvert means that you're more energized by time spent alone rather than with people. Social crowds can quickly sap the introvert of energy. There's a tendency to seek out quieter, less stimulating environments.

But that doesn't mean introverts can't put our faith into action, particularly at times of the year when we're reminded of the importance of doing so. And so I offer you the following suggestions:

WRITE. Introverts need time to think about what they want to say and how they want to say it. Writing is an ideal outlet for this kind of communication. Use correspondence to live out Jesus' Great Commandment. During the season of Advent, send one email, text, or note each day to someone you care about or admire. Tell them how you feel. Plan for bigger goals in the New Year. Start a blog! Join an online Bible study.

139

LISTEN. Introverts are gifted at listening, and their calm, gentle demeanor is the perfect balm for someone in distress. The holiday season can tap into loneliness and sadness for a lot of people. Look for opportunities to lend a listening ear to someone who needs it. A meaningful one-on-one connection allows you to be Jesus for that person, and to see Jesus in them.

PRAY. Quiet prayer comes naturally to introverts, and what better time of year to embrace the silence and stillness than Advent. Seek out moments of quiet solitude as often as you can. Try new forms of silent prayer like meditation or adoration of the Blessed Sacrament. Use this holy season to deepen your relationship with God.

BE CREATIVE. Many churches and faith communities offer opportunities for community service at this time of year. If helping others by being in the thick of the action doesn't work for you, find ways to help behind the scenes. Instead of mingling at a fundraiser, volunteer to help design the flyer or stuff envelopes. Your contribution is no less important because you weren't "in the spotlight."

STRETCH. Don't let being an introvert become an excuse. It's a huge temptation for introverts to hide away rather than engage with the world. Look for ways that God is gently challenging you to stretch out in faith.

Whether you're an introvert, an extrovert, or somewhere in between—my prayer for you this Advent season is that you will seek ways to grow in your relationship with our loving God, as we await the coming of our Savior.

The First and Greatest Gift

Every year at Christmas, I do some reminiscing about treasured gifts from my own childhood. One that always sticks in my mind is from 1978. All year I wished and hoped for the "Pretty Changes" Barbie doll. She had a series of hair extensions, hats, and accessories allowing you to change her look from day-to-day. I was filled with joy to find her under the Christmas tree, and she was by far the best gift I got that year.

Several months later, in a minor tussle with my older sister, my doll's head broke off. Feeling awful, my sister valiantly tried to glue it back on, but didn't quite get it on straight. As a result, my Barbie had a thick and stubby neck, and permanently looked smugly off to the side, never meeting the gaze of her Barbie doll friends.

I lost my enthusiasm to play with "Pretty Changes" after that. She was broken...and I had no use for broken things.

Now at Christmas time I think about another broken body, and what it means to all of us. God's sending Jesus to suffer and die a brutal death was an act of profound love. A love without tests or conditions. A love that is perfect and selfless. Beginning with the Christmas story, we celebrate this love in the breaking of the bread each time we gather for Eucharist.

God's love isn't something we receive only if we deserve it.
It's a gift freely given.

God's mercy isn't something we have to earn.
It's a gift freely given.

God's grace isn't something we have to work for.
It's a gift freely given.

When a child is born, parents experience a new and deeper kind of love—a love that consumes their entire being. This is but a fraction of the love God has for us. I got a Christmas card a few years ago. On the front of the card was a picture of the sweet and cuddly Baby Jesus. On the inside was a picture of the broken body of Jesus on the cross...crown of thorns on his head and nails piercing his hands and feet. Broken and beautiful. The inscription read: "Jesus was God's most extravagant gift."

For God so loved the world that he gave his only Son,
so that everyone who believes in him may not perish but
may have eternal life.
JOHN 3:16

As we move into January, all ornaments, garland, and glittery baubles are safely packed away for another year. What remains is the GIFT. The first and greatest gift any of us will ever receive.

How will you use that gift?

PART TEN:

SEASONAL REFLECTIONS: LENT AND EASTER

I am the resurrection and the life. The one who believes in me will live, even though they die; and whoever lives by believing in me will never die.

JOHN 11:25-26

Sacred Struggle – Journeying through the Desert

My parish choir sang a hymn on Ash Wednesday that described Lent as a "sacred struggle." What a beautiful and thought-provoking phrase! It suggests that Lent is not a time for putting up a front of spiritual tranquility. It's not a time for pretending everything is rosy and perfect. Think of Lent as a pilgrimage—a journey—and not necessarily an easy one. It's time to dig deep. To walk in the desert with Jesus.

Jesus was led by the Holy Spirit out into the parched wilderness to be tempted, tested and prepared, just as the ancient Israelites wandered the desert so many years before, in preparation for their entry into the Promised Land. We are called to make this same 40-day journey. To be tested, prepared, and renewed. To encounter God in new ways. And to ultimately be transformed by the experience.

Let us approach this Lenten season as an opportunity to embrace that which is difficult. To face temptations. To examine our personal failings. To reveal our doubts. To work through blocks and barriers to our faith.

Don't be afraid to walk through the desert. You are not alone in the journey. When you encounter thirst and drought, cry out to God to quench your spirit. Know, without a doubt, that God will answer. "They were not thirsty when he led them through the deserts; he divided the rock, and water gushed out for them to drink" (Isaiah 48:21).

A desert journey is not a time of punishment, but a time of strengthening. Jesus left his time in the wilderness with a renewed and strengthened spirit to begin preaching the message that the Kingdom of Heaven was near (Matthew 4:17). Your time in the desert will lead you closer to that Kingdom. To a place of deeper connection to our Divine Creator. To a greater understanding of the gifts we receive—brought to fruition with the Resurrection of our Lord on Easter Sunday.

May your Lenten journey be blessed, as you come out of the desert with a renewed spirit. Amen.

A Woman's Lenten Journey

The season of Lent is a journey. A journey to the foot of the cross at Calvary...and to the heart of Jesus.

Years of working in retreat ministry has shown me that more than anything, women long for a daily encounter with God. Whatever form that may take, the desire to connect with the Divine is a major driver in a woman's spiritual journey. When I was on retreat many years ago, the speaker gave us the following advice: *"Don't ever be satisfied with where you are with God at this moment. Always desire something deeper."*

Reaching for that "something deeper" can be a real challenge. Today's woman is pulled in a million different directions. Always on the go, we are doers and nurturers. This hectic pace can make it very difficult to listen for the voice of God. Women need time! We need quiet. We need a safe, sacred space, free from distraction. We need to stand still long enough to be found. Only then can we take up our cross once again and resume the journey.

When my son started middle school, he had a hard time dealing with the stress of a more demanding academic schedule. He was a serious student and became easily stressed out and overwhelmed by the amount of homework he had. When I saw him getting anxious, I would suggest that we take a "Quiet Moment." He would lay on his bed with the lights off and play a soft piece of music on his headphones. It only took about five minutes, but it did a great job of calming him down, restoring him, and helping him get back to work.

To get the most out of each Lenten season, I urge you to follow my son's example and take a Quiet Moment every day. Sit in a comfortable spot. Listen to some soft music. Give yourself totally and completely to the quiet, the stillness, and the promise of the Risen Lord. If you can only spare a few minutes, that will be enough.

The season of Lent is a journey. May your journey be blessed as you find that "something deeper" in the loving arms of our merciful God.

God's Work in Progress

Christians often refer to the season of Lent as a second chance at our New Year's resolutions. Our broken January promises are renewed as we vow to give up unhealthy foods, to take on healthier habits, to change in some significant way. For the most part, I love this time of year because it ushers in a season of transformation and renewal, as we embrace growth and progress. But there are some "side effects" of this approach that can actually halt our progress in two significant ways if we're not careful.

1. A constant focus on all the many ways we need "fixing" can become a roadblock on our spiritual journey, causing us to hold ourselves back from God because of this belief that we are not good enough.

2. Our efforts to do it all ourselves as we choose and control our own path to change can get in the way of God's plans for us.

On both January 1ˢᵗ and Ash Wednesday, I always used to say: "I'm a work in progress. There's a LOT of work I need to do." Somewhere along the way I reframed this statement:

I am God's work in progress, and God is working in me.

The best way to make this shift in our thinking is to begin with pondering our own creation. God created us from the dust and breathed life into us. He created us in His own image. That is no small thing!! Our very existence is an intimate act of union with our Creator.

> *You saw me before I was born and scheduled each day of my life before I began to breathe. Every day was recorded in your book!*
>
> PSALM 139:16

God knows us better than anyone. God lives in us. God has a plan for our lives that is unfolding each and every day. As much as we are programmed to take control and be the captain of our own ship, we need to cooperate with God's plan for us. By listening. By letting Him in. By letting Him do the work. One of my favorite metaphors for God comes from Isaiah:

> *Yet you, Lord, are our Father. We are the clay, you are the potter; we are all the work of your hand.*
>
> ISAIAH 64:8

God will mold us into what He knows we can be. It isn't always going to be easy. But then again, what prize truly worth having comes easily? My dear friend Barbara once told me about a method of sculpting called "cut and slam" in which a piece of clay is cut into two pieces and one piece is slammed on top of the other. This process is repeated over and over until the clay is ready for sculpting. Not exactly a gentle experience for the clay, but necessary. And when the sculpting is complete, the result is something new and beautiful. It is the same for us when we experience struggle or challenges in our lives. We are being molded in ways that are necessary for our growth. We are God's masterpiece. Always a work in progress, we have to allow God to move in us if we want to grow.

During this Lenten season, I invite you to ponder the ways in which you are God's work in progress.

Jesus' Last Lecture

A college professor is invited to give a hypothetical "last lecture" in which they answer the question: "If this is the last lecture you would ever give to your students, what would you say?" The professor is challenged with the task of packing in decades of wisdom and life lessons into one hour. In 2007, Randy Pausch, a professor of Computer Science at Carnegie Mellon University, was invited to do just that. What was uniquely moving about this lecture, was that Pausch was dying of pancreatic cancer. His talk, entitled "Really Achieving Your Childhood Dreams," was delivered to a packed house of over 400 colleagues and students. This lecture became the basis for the New York Times best-selling book, *The Last Lecture*, co-authored by Pausch and published in 2008. It became his legacy to his children before he died in that same year.

During Holy Week, I invite you to spend some time reading Jesus' "Last Lecture" (John 13-17). It was the day before Passover and Jesus, knowing that the hour had come for him to leave this world, gathered his disciples one last time. He washed their feet, in a beautiful example of how they were to minister to one another after he was gone.

And then He began to speak. "Dear children, how brief are these moments before I must go away and leave you!" (John 13:33). I imagine the sense of urgency Jesus must have felt as He tried one last time to impart everything He wanted His disciples to learn before He would leave them.

For four and a half chapters of John's Gospel—often referred to as the "Last Supper Discourse" or the "Farewell Discourse"—Jesus gives His disciples instructions, life lessons, and final words of wisdom. There's so much rich and wonderful content in His words, it could never be covered in one short essay. (It reads like a "Greatest Hits" of Bible quotes!) So I've chosen seven lines from Jesus' Last Lecture—one for each day of Holy Week—for you to ponder and pray about:

MONDAY

"A new command I give you: Love one another. As I have loved you, so you must love one another. By this everyone will know that you are my disciples, if you love one another" (John 13:34-35). This is it...really. The entirety of Jesus' ministry and message summed up in one commandment. Love one another. During this holiest week of the year, how will we choose to love one another?

TUESDAY

"I am the way and the truth and the life. No one comes to the Father except through me" (John 14:6). One of my favorite lines in all of Scripture! Jesus tells his disciples that he is going to prepare a place for them in his Father's house. Thomas replies: "Lord, we do not know where you are going; so how can we know the way to get there?" The answer is simple and profound. Jesus is the WAY. Our guide and our bridge to God and the Promised Land. All we need to do is follow Him.

WEDNESDAY

"If you love me, keep my commands. And I will ask the Father, and he will give you another advocate to help you and be with you forever—the Spirit of truth. The world cannot accept him, because it neither sees him nor knows him. But you know him, for he lives with you and will be in you" (John 14:15-17). In this passage we learn about the Holy Spirit. Jesus promises his disciples that they will never be left alone, a promise that still holds for us today. The Holy Spirit is an Advocate or Helper that dwells within us forever...to comfort, guide, and lead us.

THURSDAY

"Peace I leave with you; my peace I give you. I do not give to you as the world gives. Do not let your hearts be troubled and do not be afraid" (John 14:27). Yet another beautiful gift from our Savior. Peace, not as the world gives—based on outward circumstances—but peace from within. Peace that is rooted in absolute trust in the faithfulness of God. A gift that becomes ours only in the act of receiving. How will we receive the peace of Christ this week?

FRIDAY

"I am the vine; you are the branches. If you remain in me and I in you, you will bear much fruit; apart from me you can do nothing." (John 15:5) In these beautiful words we see Jesus' message of discipleship. We are meant to bear fruit...to spread the love of Christ like branches stretching out from a vine. But we must remain connected to the source of our creation. Our dependence on God allows us to become an instrument of His love and peace.

SATURDAY

"My command is this: Love each other as I have loved you. There is no greater love than to lay down one's life for one's friends" (John 15:12-13). After once again repeating his central commandment, Jesus foreshadows the great act of sacrifice that is to come on Good Friday. Jesus dying on the cross is an act of profound love. One that transforms the disciples to such a degree that they passionately preach His message, even to the point of their own deaths in martyrdom. How will we let Jesus transform us during this Easter season? How can we "die" to our own self-absorption in order to live renewed in Christ?

SUNDAY

"I have told you these things, so that in me you may have peace. In this world you will have trouble. But take heart! I have overcome the world" (John 16:33). The sorrow of the crucifixion and death of Jesus give way to the victory and triumph of Easter morning. We are born to new life in Christ. Alleluia, He is Risen!

You Are Loved

When I was an 18-year-old college freshman, a chaplain at my school, Fr. Michael Ford. S.J., said the following words during a homily that have stayed with me all these years:

"Expect to be loved and be loving in return."

Back then I was young and filled with insecurities. It felt a bit presumptuous to expect to be loved. Who was I, after all, to be worthy of such love?

It reminded me of something a friend said not long ago. We were talking about a love song that was playing on the radio. Assuming the artist wrote the song for his real-life spouse, my friend exclaimed: "How lucky this person is...to be loved like that!" Beneath her words was the subtle implication that she didn't feel loved in this all-encompassing way.

I heard about a recent survey looking at happiness and well-being in adults, and 17 percent of all respondents said that they did not feel loved. How heartbreaking! I wish I could have found each and every one of that 17 percent and told them how wrong they were.

The journey of Lent and its culmination in the Resurrection on Easter Sunday shows us in the most profound way that we ARE loved.

> *For God so loved the world that he gave his one and only Son, that whoever believes in him shall not perish but have eternal life.*
> JOHN 3:16

We were created to be loved by God. In his book, *Life of the Beloved*, Henri Nouwen describes it in the following way: *"Long before any human being saw us, we are seen by God's loving eyes. Long before anyone heard us cry or laugh, we are heard by our God who is all ears for us. Long before any person spoke to us in this world, we are spoken to by the voice of eternal love."*

And then we turn our thoughts to the second part of Fr. Ford's advice—"be loving in return." When Jesus gathered his disciples at the Last Supper he gave them this directive: "A new command I give you: Love one another. As I have loved you, so you must love one another" (John 13:34). Parable after parable teaches us that we must love one another.

Yes—being born into God's love comes with responsibility. One that we should welcome. Sometimes I think our world has become less good at loving. People are defined as winners and losers rather than brothers and sisters. Cruelty prevails over compassion. Bigotry overshadows our shared humanity. This is not what God hoped for when he breathed life into our souls. It's not what Jesus wanted when he commanded us to love one another.

I invite and encourage you to reflect on Fr. Ford's words during this season of Lent: *"Expect to be loved and be loving in return."* How will you acknowledge God's great love for you? How will you share God's love with others?

Prayers
for
Everyday Grace

The feeling remains that God
is on the journey, too.

St. Teresa of Avila

A Breathing Prayer

I breathe.

Lord God, You gave me the breath of life
A Divine Spark moving within
Dawning awareness that I am Your beloved child

I breathe deeply.

Emmanuel...You are with me
Abiding in me and around me and through me
Surrounding me with extravagant love and mercy

I breathe slowly.

Jesus, You are my Cornerstone
A firm foundation to cling to when worry and fear
Threaten to steal the breath from my body

I breathe in and out.

I am drawn into Your presence, Loving God
Welling up with peace, love, and grace
Until You are ALL in ALL

I breathe in Your Holy Presence.

AMEN.

Refresh Me, Remind Me, Release Me

Lord, there are days when my prayer life stagnates. When the old trusty prayers fail to inspire. When new words won't come. Everything is dry as the desert. On these days, I ask you to come to me in a new way. Help me discover fresh ways to see you, to talk with you, to know you. Refresh my desert days with living water.

Lord, there are days when I forget to pray at all. When signs of you are all around me, but I fail to see them. Instead my mind focuses on the endless "to do" list. The daily distractions of the outer world. On these days, I ask you to send me a reminder of your loving presence. Help me to see your authorship in all that surrounds me. Guide me from my wandering with a gentle reminder.

Lord, there are days when I find myself stuck. Clenching my fist tightly around a past hurt or a stubborn mindset. This holding on becomes a holding back. On these days, I ask you to grant me permission to let go. Release me from all that holds me in chains. So that I might move forward in love and action and inspiration.

AMEN.

A Prayer of Receiving

We pray in wonder and awe for Creation, your ancient gift of grace. You made the sun and moon, the land and seas, and all the creatures of the earth. You created us in your own image as your beloved sons and daughters. Today we reflect on your gift of precious life here on earth.

Open our hearts, O Lord, to receive your gift of amazing grace.

We pray in wonder and awe for your gift of grace—fulfilled in your Son, Jesus Christ, who suffered death on a cross that we might live. In mercy, you gave us your Son to pay ransom for all our sins. Today we reflect on your gift of everlasting life.

Open our hearts, O Lord, to receive your gift of amazing grace.

We pray in thanksgiving for the blessings you grant us. Your grace is not something we must earn or deserve. It is a gift freely given. We pray in thanksgiving for your extravagant love. Like the compassionate father, you welcome us home when we are lost. Your redeeming grace rescues us from a life of darkness.

Open our hearts, O Lord, to receive your gift of amazing grace.

We promise to seek you in sanctuary. In the quiet stillness, we hear you speak to us. In your loving embrace, we are restored. We promise to seek you in the everyday moments of ordinary life. To pray where we are and invite you into each moment. Through this ongoing conversation, with you we receive peace and contentment.

Open our hearts, O Lord, to receive your gift of amazing grace.

Give us new eyes to see the beauty of Your creation, new ears to listen for Your whispers, and a new outlook to experience the transforming power of Your love.

AMEN.

Images of God

God is Light
Loving God, be my LIGHT
Source of my innermost being
Illuminating my path
Dispelling the darkness
Shining in the faces of the least of my brothers and sisters

Loving God, be my SHEPHERD
Bringing me to safety
Guiding me and leading me home
Whether one or one hundred
I am found

Loving God, be my ROCK
Safety and permanence
Ancient presence
Providing stability to cling to when the world tilts and swirls
You cannot be moved

Loving God, be my LIVING WATER
Refreshing streams flowing over dry, cracked earth
Quenching my thirst when I wander through the desert
Washing me clean with gentle mercy
The source of life in You

AMEN.

Lost and Found

Loving God, bless the times when I am a seeker. Forever seeking to know you more deeply. Traveling to all places and all times to discover you in our midst. I seek those thin places where the veil between heaven and earth is lifted and I can gaze upon your face.

Loving God, bless the times when I grow weary of seeking. When I simply want to be found. Come and seek me wherever I am, whatever I may be doing. When you are part of the ordinary moments of my day...then I am home.

Loving God, whether I am seeking or sought, lost or found...I praise you in all things. Your love is mighty and good. Your power is everlasting.

AMEN.

Near or Far

There are times when I see you through a thick fog.
My eyes squint and strain...but you don't take shape.
I want to BELIEVE you are near
But you seem far away.

There are days when I hear you through a
pounding rain or a crashing sea.
I lean towards you...but your voice is faint.
I must HOPE you are near
But you sound far away.

There are moments when I feel you through a crowd,
They press and pull on me from every direction.
Feeling off balance and unsteady...I don't know how
or where to reach for you.
I need to TRUST you are near
But you feel far away.

Loving God,
Emerge from the fog
Sing through the storm
Touch my heart through the chaos
I will turn my eyes and ears—my whole being—towards you.

The fog still surrounds me, the waves crash,
and the crowd presses.
But I am safe and strong—with YOU.
I can sweep the fog away. I can swallow the rain.
I can embrace the crowd.

You are near...you are HERE, always.

AMEN.

I am the Lord Your God

Blessed be God who frees us from all burdens

That which holds me prisoner—
Lord, you are MIGHTY with breaking these chains

That which presses on my soul—
Lord, you are STRONG with compassion to take my yoke upon you

Blessed be God who keeps His promises

That which holds me back from the Promised Land
Lord, you are FAITHFUL with promises kept—

That which keeps me lost in the desert—
Lord, you are PATIENT with teaching me your paths

Blessed be God who comes to us with outstretched arms

That which leaves me weak—
Lord, you are STRONG with my name written
on the palm of your Hand

That which brings me to the foot of your Cross—
Lord, you are STEADFAST with love that endures forever

AMEN.

A Morning Prayer
(Inspired by 1 Samuel 3:10)

Speak Lord, your servant is listening;
What is it that you ask of me this day?

Speak Lord, your servant is listening;
Wake me from my slumber with your gentle calling.

Speak Lord, your servant is listening;
Who is it that you wish me to serve today?

Speak Lord, your servant is listening;
Reveal yourself to me.

Speak Lord, your servant is listening;
Where will send me on this day?

Speak Lord, your servant is listening;
Here I am! Set me on the right path.

Speak Lord, your servant is listening;
When will you answer?

Speak Lord, your servant is listening;
Work in me and through me...in your own time.

AMEN.

A Prayer for the Present Moment

Loving God, I come to you as I am,
Rushed and frazzled, electricity buzzing from my fingertips,
Or sluggish, plodding through the mud, footsteps heavy and slow.
Whatever my pace, I have arrived at this precise moment with you.

Lord Jesus, I rest in the knowledge that you will meet me here,
At the crossroads of sorrow and joy,
Of confusion and clarity,
Of stress and serenity.

Heavenly Father, help me to pause.
To listen, and pray, and sit in the quiet
With you, my song blending with yours
In beautiful harmony

God of love, I pray for the inspiration to put away my own plans,
And discover what you have in mind for me
I am listening, I am here with you.
I will be present.
I will just BE.

AMEN.

A Prayer for Everyday Grace

Lord, I bring to you all that is on my plate. The noise, the clutter, the chaos, and the distractions. Help me to empty myself so that I may see you, hear you, and feel your presence. Empty the interior space of my soul that I may receive you and discover who I truly am.

Lord, I bring to you my fears and worries...all the things that are so heavy and hard to carry. I place them into your hands. Loving God, may your Spirit come to move my life. I place my trust and faith in you.

Lord, I bring to you my burdens. Things that I cannot control weigh me down like a heavy stone. On the days that I am tired, stressed, and weary, I know that you walk with me. I know that you are my Rock—my Cornerstone—and I can find rest in you.

Lord, I bring to you a heart that longs for healing. I know that when I choose to sin, I separate myself from you. Help me to remember that because of the sacrifice of your Son, Jesus Christ, there are no longer any walls between us. Grant me wisdom to make good choices and the courage to seek to be reconciled with you when I do not. Help me to forgive myself and others as you have forgiven me.

Open my heart, O Lord, to receive your gift of amazing grace!

AMEN.

A Prayer for Today
(Inspired by Psalm 139)

Dear God, I thank you for making me wonderfully unique. You knit together my talents, my flaws, my moods, and my dreams. At the moment of my creation you were there, loving me beyond measure. You know what it is that I need for this day and for this season. You provide me with abundant blessings and gifts to meet each challenge with love and patience.

On the days when I can't seem to get anything right...You are there, holding me gently.

On the days when I can't stop comparing myself to those who are smarter, better, thinner, or just MORE...You are there, reminding me that I am your Beloved Child.

On the days when stress, fear, doubt, and worry threaten to stop me in my tracks...You are there, gently nudging me forward.

On the days when words don't seem adequate to thank you, to praise you, to glorify your name...You are there, understanding the prayers that spill from my heart.

Dear Lord, help me to listen to what it is that you ask of me today and in this season. Let me live and act with compassion and kindness. Help me to love boldly. Guide me in following the example of your Son, Jesus Christ, in all that I do and say.

AMEN.

What Makes Your Life Full?

The essence of wisdom is remembering what we already know.
So what is it that we already know?

We know that God is always with us.
But do we REMEMBER to feel his loving presence
during difficult times?

We know how important it is to spend quiet time in prayer.
Do we REMEMBER to break from our hectic schedules
to pray or sit in the stillness?

We know that God called us from the womb,
a precious creation in his own image.
Do we REMEMBER to value ourselves as gift?

We know that Jesus died for us.
Do we REMEMBER to reflect on the enormity
of that sacrifice and what it means for us?

Life is FULL of distractions, interruptions,
interferences, disruptions.
We say we're busy, chaotic, hectic, frenzied.

Life is FULL of the unforeseen, the unpredictable,
the unexpected, the unplanned.
We get pulled away, wrapped up, preoccupied, sidetracked.

REMEMBER how much God loves you.
REMEMBER that God is always waiting for you.
REMEMBER all of this...

And your life will be FULL indeed!

Journeying in Faith

I pray for the strength of Abraham.
How difficult it is for me to set off not knowing where I am going.
I am always one for charting the course ahead.
For knowing exactly what to expect.
But only you know what lies in store for me.
And I must have faith if I am to receive my inheritance.

I pray for the certainty of Abraham.
Just as he looked forward to a new city in a new land,
Help me look forward to this unseen future,
Knowing that you are its architect and builder.
And you are mighty!

I pray for the faith of Abraham.
He knew hopelessness and despair, as he yearned for a child
Though he was old and his wife was barren.
But you blessed Abraham and Sarah with a child.
Not just one—descendants to number the stars in the sky!
Bless my new journey, let it bear the fruits of your glory.

Loving God, bless me as you blessed your chosen one, Abraham
Teach me your paths and guide me in your ways
Let all that I do reflect your love, mercy, and compassion
For my faith lies in you.

AMEN.

Love Enough

Loving God,
The day draws nearer
when my children will fly out into the world.
To discover, to fall, to grow, to cry
To choose, to lose their way, to find it again.

Fear grips my heart with icy fingers
What if...they choose wrong?
What if...they fall hard?
What if...they do not find their way?

I want to hold them back,
gripping them with my own icy fingers
Hands that used to let go all the time
Taking first steps, riding a bike, getting on the school bus
Why is it so hard this time?

Have I done enough?
Have I prepared them...enough?
Have I taught them...enough?
Will I ever be ready...enough?

I sigh a little
And cry a little
And pray a lot.

And then one thought echoes in my frightened, restless mind.
"Do not be afraid."
And I remember
What I have always known.

They are in **YOUR** hands
And that is enough.

AMEN.

A Sinking Heart

There are times we move through life with our hearts on our sleeves. Wide open to receive God's amazing love. Moved to listen and understand, we are part of the vast family of the children of God. We offer prayers of gratitude for belonging. We reach out to our sisters and brothers in loving communion.

With our hearts on our sleeves...we sing, we laugh, and we love.

There are times that our hearts curl inward. Nestled deep within our souls. We enter into a period of searching and deep contemplation. Our hearts are wrapped in mystery. We long to hear God's whisper. We know there is something God wants to teach us and we cling to the quiet so we may uncover His truth.

With our hearts drawn in...we listen, we pray, and we learn.

And still other times our hearts just sink. We are lost in the fragments of a broken world. Hope eludes us, and despair overwhelms us. We cannot imagine a world in which God is present and working for good. Our rational minds tell us that God is out there, but with plummeting hearts we cannot see Him.

With our hearts in the depths...we doubt, we cry, and we ache.

If our hearts are going to sink, let them sink into God. Not an out-of-control free fall, but a falling in faith. This act of surrender will bring us closer to God than ever before. We give up our pain, our flaws, and our doubts, confident that God is strong enough to bear it all. The further we allow ourselves to fall, the higher God will lift us up.

If our hearts are going to sink...let them sink into God.

A Prayer for this Day

There will come a day...

When words are not used like knives, to cut down and decrease.

When the meek and lowly are raised up and valued as God's treasure.

When all weapons are cleared from the land, melted down in a mighty fire of peace.

When the poor dine on milk and honey and dignity.

When freedom is not reserved for a privileged few, but **ALL**.

There will come a day...but it is not yet this day.

This day
We turn to our God for guidance
To shine Holy light on human weakness and injustice;

To raise up prophets and soldiers
of peace and love;

To forge us with the fire of equality and grandeur,
until we are strong like steel.

Raise up
Shine down
Speak truth
Dig deep
All in all

Loving God,
Show us the way
On this day.

AMEN.

What Should I Pray?

Dear God, I'm not quite sure what to say to you today.
Is it ok with you if I don't say anything?
Can I just be aware of your presence?
Will that be enough?

I picture you out there.
It's comforting, but you're not as close
as I'd like you to be.
Can I picture you within me instead?

A spark of life deep down inside
Offering answers, hope, love, and comfort.
A tiny spark to be sure, but it's there.
Let me just sit with this knowledge for today.
That your spark lies within me.

I don't need to go outside of myself searching for it.
I don't need to sift through the rubble
of broken hearts, bigotry, violence,
and judgment to find you.

You abide in me, offering me
all that I know is true and right.
Maybe what feels like my intuition is really you,
telling me what you wish and dream for me.
I can follow that if I know it's you.

AMEN.

One Seed

The kingdom of God starts small
What is small?

Individual acts of compassion
A courageous speaking out against injustice
A kind word, a sweet smile
One meal for someone who is hungry

One act
One word
One smile
One meal
Surely one is not too much to ask

One pebble tossed into a pond
Creates ripples that grow outward and onward
Creeping
Spreading
Growing
Until one is not small but ALL

A more compassionate people
A world free from injustice
A resounding chorus of loving words
Beaming smiles reflecting peace in our world
Abundant nourishment for all who hunger

Loving God
If you will plant—I will sow
A tiny seed of love growing strong within my heart
Until I am a mighty branch
Unshakable
Providing shade for the least and last of God's children

AMEN.

Be Still

Be still and know that I am God.

Mighty God, all I need to do is look at your marvelous and audacious act of creation to know that you are God. Light and day. Land and sky. Seed and stars. Bird and lion. You created us from dust and breathed life into us. In your image you created us. Help me always remember this first and ancient moment of connection with you, my Divine Creator.

Be still and know that I am.

Loving God, when Moses approached your glory at the burning bush, he asked for your name. You responded simply "I AM." Isn't that just like you! Giving Moses a name that is not really a name. Be with me during those times that you are mysterious and hard to know. Do not remain a hidden God. Draw me close to you in intimacy and companionship.

Be still and know.

Infinite God, I know that my human brain cannot begin to comprehend all that you are. Help me to know you. Reveal yourself to me in your Word, in those around me, and in all of creation. Infuse me with the spark of realization that you are All in All.

Be still.

Patient God, being still is not easy for me. I have no problems stilling my body, but my mind is another story. Racing thoughts about what must be done, what must be worried over, what must be controlled and managed. Help me sink into the quiet, like a green meadow or a peaceful stream. Let the stillness become a new way for me to hear you. Whispering to me. Calling my name. Singing me a love song.

Be.

You breathed life in me so many years ago so I could **BE**. Not do, or accomplish, or fret, or undertake, or organize, or control. Just **BE**. Give me a glimpse of your heavenly dream for me. Help me be according to your will.

AMEN.

WORKS CITED

Budd, Luann. *Journal Keeping: Writing for Spiritual Growth.* InterVarsity Press, 2002.

Brother Lawrence. *The Practice of the Presence of God; & The Spiritual Maxims.* Benton Press, 2017.

Holmes, Marjorie. *Two from Galilee: The Story of Mary and Joseph.* Bantam Books, 1974.

MacDonald, Heather, and Pamela S. Ward. *An Almost Holy Picture: Freely Drawn from Pamela Ward's Story "The Hairy Little Girl".* Dramatists Play Service, 2004.

McClellan, O.S.B., Keith. *Prayer Therapy.* Abbey Press, 1990.

Nouwen, Henri. *Life of the Beloved.* The Crossroad Publishing Company, 1992.

Pausch, Randy, and Jeffrey Zaslow. *The Last Lecture.* Hyperion, 2008.

Wright, Vinita Hampton. *Days of Deepening Friendship: For the Woman Who Wants Authentic Life with God.* Loyola Press, 2009.

ACKNOWLEDGMENTS

I owe special thanks to Annie Mariano, who co-created Hearing God's Whisper retreat ministry with me. I never would have answered God's call to serve in this way if it weren't for her. I thank Sr. Theresina Scully, C.P. for giving me a spiritual home at Our Lady of Calvary Retreat Center so many years ago and encouraging me to explore this passion for writing and presenting retreats.

The stories I post on my blog come from my everyday experiences, and I owe special thanks to God's messengers in my life who have inspired many of the stories in this book: Cheri, Pam, Barbara, Rebecca, Carolyn, Paula, Jen, Janice, Francesca, Manny, Tony, and many more.

My retreat ministry grew organically over time, and I have many to thank for inviting me to present at parishes and retreat centers: Noranne Wamester, Kelly Henderschedt, Jen O'Neill, Mary Welch, Sr. Mary Ann Strain, C.P., Paula Daisey and Marla Rapini, Nicole Perone, Shannon Bielaczyc, Viney Wilson, Jane Staszowski, Roberta Hardt, Stephanie Haines, and Patsy Glenn, and others. Each experience enriched my faith in ways that cannot be measured.

I want to thank my parents, Joe and Judy, my sisters, Lisa, Kelly, and Ann Marie, and my siblings-in-law, Susan, Jim, and John, for their love and encouragement over the years. Special thanks to "Mommom," my beloved grandmother in heaven. How I wish she were here to hold this book in her hands!

I married into a wonderful family and I am so thankful for my mother and father-in-law, Bob and Maureen, my siblings-in-law, Matt and Rachel, and dear Nana in heaven, proof that you can never have enough family to love.

I want to thank my adoring and adored husband Mark, for encouraging me, loving me, inspiring me, and for editing every word of this book. I could not have asked for a better partner in marriage, parenting, writing, and life.

And finally, I thank my boys, Charlie and Alex. I could write ten thousand pages about them, and it would not begin to capture the sheer amount of joy and light they bring into my life every single day.

ABOUT THE AUTHOR

Sheri Dursin is a writer, speaker, and retreat presenter. She is the creator of *Hearing God's Whisper*, a blog that features her own spiritual reflections, poems, and prayers. She was also the creator of Women, Wisdom, and the Word, a faith-sharing group for women at her home parish. Since then she has facilitated numerous prayer groups and retreats, offering women and men of all ages the opportunity to come away to a safe, sacred space to reflect on the ways in which God whispers to us through the ordinary moments of our everyday lives.

Sheri is also an author of young adult fiction, and in 2017 she and her husband Mark published a YA fantasy novel called *Labors of an Epic Punk*, a retelling of Homer's Odyssey from the point of view of Odysseus' teenage son. Their book was awarded a 2018 Moonbeam Children's Book Award.

www.hearinggodswhisper.com

Made in United States
North Haven, CT
10 March 2022

16992087R00107